Doing
God

MARK D. CHAPMAN

Doing

God

*Religion and Public Policy in
Brown's Britain*

DARTON · LONGMAN + TODD

First published in 2008 by
Darton, Longman and Todd Ltd
1 Spencer Court
140–142 Wandsworth High Street
London sw18 4JJ

ISBN-10   0-232-52744-X
ISBN-13   978-0-232-52744-5

A catalogue record for this book is available from
the British Library.

Designed and produced by Sandie Boccacci
Set in 10.75/12.75pt Bembo
Printed and bound in Great Britain by
CPI Antony Rowe, Chippenham

CONTENTS

ACKNOWLEDGEMENTS

The first four chapters of this book grew out of a 20-minute lecture to the School of Government organised by the Oxford University Department for Continuing Education. It expanded as I tried out various ideas in different places, most importantly at a conference called 'Re-moralising Britain' hosted by the Lincoln Theological Institute in Manchester in May 2007 to mark the tenth anniversary of Tony Blair becoming Prime Minister. I am grateful to Dr Peter Scott for the invitation to speak alongside some much more famous people. I am also grateful to Rowan Williams for lecturing on multiculturalism at a particularly opportune moment (which, I should add, had nothing to do with me). Chapters 5 and 6 were first presented to the applied theology seminar in Oxford in February 2008 as an attempt to contextualise what he said at the Royal Courts of Justice. I am particularly grateful to him for making time in his hectic schedule to read what I wrote about him and for being so gracious in his response. It is a great tragedy that there seem to be so many in the Anglican Communion and elsewhere who seem to be unaware of the greatness and profundity of their archbishop. Several other people read these chapters and made helpful comments, including my friend and colleague, Martyn Percy, and the wonderfully hospitable Michael Brierley. Unfortunately, I doubt that Gordon Brown and his colleagues in government will make space in their busy diaries to read this book, but if they do, I hope that they would at least understand what I am trying to say, and even that they might heed my advice.

MARK D. CHAPMAN
St George's Day, 2008

CHAPTER ONE

On Not Doing God

Shortly before the May 2005 General Election I published a book called *Blair's Britain: A Christian Critique* which offered an assessment of the eight years or so of the policies of the New Labour Government from a Christian perspective. I did not aim to be comprehensive, but instead I offered a few connected reflections on some of the key aspects of the policies of the New Labour Government. I concentrated on a detailed discussion of the problems of managerialism and centralisation, as well as the nature of 'community' which was central to many of the Government's policies. My recommendations for public policy in the final chapter were somewhat ill-defined and were perhaps too vague to be of much practical use – something which some of the critics noted. I was probably better at criticising the Government than at offering constructive ways forward, which may be a trait of my kind of personality type. This book is a sort of sequel to *Blair's Britain*, but whereas I tackled a whole range of public policy in that book, in this book I have chosen instead to focus on religion. This might seem to be of marginal interest – after all, most British people are not actively religious, and increasing numbers have little awareness of either

Christianity or of any of the other world religions represented in Britain. Nevertheless, as I will show, religion is so
central to many aspects of public policy that it simply cannot
be ignored. Particularly since the atrocities of 11 September
2001 in New York and Washington, and even more after the
London bombings of 7 July 2005, which killed fifty-two
commuters as well as the four suicide bombers, religion –
especially Islam – has seldom been off the political agenda.

The unprecedented terrorist phenomenon of home-
grown suicide bombers suddenly erupted onto the British
political scene the day after London had won the bid to host
the 2012 Olympic Games. The bombers included apparently
upstanding citizens who had invested in the British system,
including Mohammad Sidique Khan, who was born in
Leeds and lived in Dewsbury, and had worked as a teaching
assistant. He had even helped organise a local cricket team.
He recorded a videotape in which he claimed to speak in
the name of Islam, and against the democratically elected
governments, which 'continuously perpetuate atrocities
against my people all over the world'.[1] While obviously this
is not typical of the opinions of the average Muslim, there
is a sense in which questions of multiculturalism – and
especially the way in which religion functions in cultural
identity – have become far more urgent after 7 July. Was
there an inevitable clash of civilisations as predicted in the
popular apocalyptic rhetoric of Samuel Huntington?[2] Or
was British society capable of providing a set of simple universal values capable of assimilating even those of other
faiths? Or was the whole set of issues far more complex?[3]

In a country which has tended to regard religion as a
bit like sex – a private matter which should take place
behind closed doors – the sort of militant political religion
demonstrated in the terrorist outrages served as a rude
awakening. Secular discourse, which had dominated British
political life for so long, had little space for categorising
public religion, even in its more benign forms. Whereas in

the United States religious language has been used openly
by politicians of all hues, and where it would be difficult to
imagine an open atheist attaining highest office, British
politicians have tended to avoid explicit religious language
for a very long time. Indeed, among Prime Ministers in
modern times, it was only Gladstone who was prepared to
engage publicly in theological and religious debate, and to
draw on his faith explicitly in policy-making, perhaps most
obviously in the Bulgarian atrocities campaign of
1874–76.[4] Despite their central role in the choice of the
leadership of the Church of England, British Prime
Ministers of different parties have not been a very religious
bunch (and among this irreligious group we might include
Lloyd George, Churchill and Wilson). And even when they
have spoken of their faith commitment and have been
known as practising Christians, most politicians have been
very reticent about speaking of their faith. This is certainly
true both of Tony Blair and Gordon Brown, both of whom
have been members of the Christian Socialist Movement,
but neither of whom has said much about how faith has influenced their approach to public policy. The only leading
Labour figure of recent years who has written explicitly
about his faith at length is the idiosyncratic Frank Field,
whom I discussed in *Blair's Britain*.[5] He did not last very
long in government.

This book is about the public and political dimensions
of religion and how these relate to what is usually the
extremely secular activity of the formulation of public
policy. My contention is that human identity is conferred
by a whole range of sometimes competing associations,
which for many people, especially those from minority
ethnic and immigrant communities, will be religious. Since
identity is principally constituted by networks of public
relationships it is a serious error to see religion as primarily
a private matter. Post-Enlightenment secular discourse has
tended to regard religion as something based on private

experience and a matter of individual choice: while this may be true in part, it is only half the story. Since religion is less about beliefs and more about practices and public commitment, then it inevitably affects the ways in which people relate together politically. This means that it can never be simply a private matter. At least on this point, it seems to me, John Milbank is right. The liberal relegation of religion to a matter of private conscience rendered it impotent in the public sphere, which meant that it could exert 'no positively definable effects within the objectively factual world'.[6] For good or ill, however, religion is once more very much a public phenomenon and cannot be regarded simply as a private lifestyle choice.

At the same time, however, the secular sphere with its claims to neutrality and universality continues to dominate the political discourse of western Europe. Where a significant number of citizens do not share such a world-view, there is likely to be a degree of tension which may sometimes lead to outright conflict. Consequently, where different sets of values co-exist alongside one another, it seems imperative for politicians to grasp the importance of public religion. While it may not be the dominant discourse, it is nevertheless crucial for it to be recognised and as far as possible accommodated in any workable political settlement. This book is a preliminary attempt to analyse religion in relation to public policy. Because of the elusiveness of the characterisation of religion, I have been immediately drawn into a discussion of several related themes. The most important of these, which I discuss at length in Chapter 2, is that of 'community', particularly 'community cohesion' (discussed in detail in Chapter 4), which is intimately connected to that of religion, and which takes the discussion of *Blair's Britain* much further. Chapter 3 relates this theme to 'multiculturalism' and the idea of Britishness. In Chapters 5 and 6, I take up the theme of Islam and Christianity and how they relate to the 'national' community, drawing on the ideas of 'interactive pluralism' developed by Rowan Williams, Archbishop of Canterbury. In a brief conclusion, I outline some tentative policy proposals which take further some of the suggestions of the final chapter of *Blair's Britain*.

On not doing God: Gordon Brown

The relegation of religion to the private sphere can be illustrated clearly from an analysis of the religious views of the present and past occupants of 10 Downing St. On 27 June 2007 Gordon Brown became Prime Minister of the United Kingdom. Nobody could have been very surprised, especially after Tony Blair had announced the previous summer that he would resign before the next general election. Indeed, there was an air of expectation in the media about what Gordon Brown would be like as Prime Minister almost from the time of Blair's successful re-election to Downing Street for his third term in May 2005. It hardly needs to be pointed out that Gordon Brown has a very different public persona from that of his predecessor. When he succeeded to office he was almost universally greeted as a 'son of the manse', that is, an earnest Scottish Presbyterian type with a distinct lack of a sense of humour (although few journalists showed much awareness of the Church of Scotland, and a number called his father a 'parish priest'). His father, John Ebenezer Brown, was minister of St Brycedale Church in Kirkcaldy. The dour Calvinist image, however, has been questioned by virtually all of Gordon Brown's friends, who remember him as a highly intelligent, extremely driven, and prodigiously untidy character who succeeded in virtually everything he did. In the early months of the New Labour Government Brown distanced himself from his Presbyterian roots, claiming that he found Calvinism a 'very black religion'. He did not find appealing the 'idea that it doesn't matter what you do, that you could be predetermined for damnation'.[7]

[5]

In a detailed recent discussion of Brown's speeches, the practical theologian Doug Gay has shown that there is almost a complete absence of Calvinist and Presbyterian vocabulary, and instead a dependence on the language of the Scottish Enlightenment, especially that of that other famous son of Kirkcaldy, Adam Smith. Brown's faith has been privatised, although there is a public role given to the churches in terms of the creation of social capital.[8] In short, writes Gay:

> Brown is markedly less willing than Blair to challenge the 'hard secularism' of Labour and the liberal intelligentsia – in his public persona he is the quintessential, modernist, demythologised, liberal *kultur*Presbyterian with little if any red-blooded Calvinism in his veins. Sure, the stereotypes will still cling, but there is little sign so far of any intellectual or theological substance to them.[9]

Gay is accurate in his assessment of Brown, at least in his reluctance to speak of his personal faith. While acknowledging that he was influenced by his religious upbringing, Brown has preferred to steer clear of specific religious language. 'Being brought up as the son of a minister,' he said in an early interview, 'made me aware of community responsibilities that any decent society ought to accept. And strong communities remain the essential bedrock for individual prosperity.'[10] Similarly, he claimed, 'as a minister's son you see every problem coming to your doorstep. You become aware of a whole range of distress and social problems. I suppose it's not a bad training for politics.'[11] On one of the few occasions where he mentioned the sort of Christianity taught by his father, Brown said in the mid 1990s that his father was

> more a social Christian than a fundamentalist. His sermons were about charity, good works … I was very

impressed with my father ... There was always a constant stream of people passing through our front door. As a child growing up in a minister's family, you get to see all the hardships that are going on around you at first hand. All of them had been hit hard ... I have learned a great deal from what my father managed to do for other people. He taught me to treat everyone equally and that is something I have not forgotten ... personally, my religion is built on a far greater sense of people's importance and potential.[12]

More recently, Brown has continued in much the same vein. Christianity is more about building up social capital than a specific set of doctrines:

I don't recall the sermons my father preached. But I will never forget these words he left me with: 'We must be givers as well as getters.' Put something back. And by doing so make a difference. This is my moral compass.[13]

Similarly, in his 2006 speech to the Labour Party Conference in Manchester, he claimed to have learned his values from his father, who was a minister of the Church, but who was motivated not by 'theological zeal but compassion':

He told me 'you can leave your mark on the world for good or ill'. And my mother taught my brothers and me that whatever talents we had, however small, we should use them. I don't romanticise my upbringing. But my parents were more than an influence, they were – and still are – my inspiration. The reason I am in politics. And all I believe and all I try to do comes from the values I learned from them. They believed in duty, responsibility, and respect for others. They believed in honesty and hard work, and that the things that matter had to be worked for. Most of all my

parents taught me that each of us should live by a
moral compass. It was a simple faith with a fundamental optimism. That each and every one of us has a
talent. Each of us a duty to use that talent. And each of
us should have the chance to develop that talent. And
my parents thought we should use whatever talent we
had to help people least able to help themselves ...
That's why I joined the Labour Party – out of faith –
faith in people, that they should have the opportunity
to realise their potential. And I believed then and I
believe now that at all times the Labour Party must
stand for more than a programme: we must have a
soul.[14]

Faith in people – the tradition of ethical socialism – was far
more important than faith in God: indeed, it was this that
gave the Labour Party its soul.

He repeated similar themes in his acceptance speech at
the Labour Party Conference after he had been elected
leader of the Labour Party. 'All I believe and all I try to do,'
he claimed, 'comes from the values that I grew up with:
duty, honesty, hard work, family and respect for others.' His
parents, he went on, taught him 'that each and everyone of
us has a talent, each and everyone of us should have the
chance to develop their talent, and that each of us should
use whatever talents we have to enable people least able to
help themselves.' He made the point about being what he
called a 'conviction politician', but he was careful to make
sure that his conviction was never explicitly named as
Christian:

Call it 'the driving power of social conscience', call it
'the better angels of our nature', call it 'our moral
sense', call it a belief in 'civic duty'. I joined this party
as a teenager because I believed in these values. They
guide my work, they are my moral compass. This is
who I am. And because these are the values of our

> party too the party I lead must have more than a set of
> policies – we must have a soul.[15]

That soul and those convictions, however, were never
named as Christian, at least not in public.

The reason for Brown's reluctance to speak about his
religious convictions in public is probably straightforward.
Public expressions of religion are unacceptable, especially to
the British media. As the commentator Christina Paterson
wrote in *The Independent*: 'Gordon Brown's Christianity is,
luckily, of the harder-for-a-rich-man-to-pass-through-the-
eye-of-a-needle variety, rather than the God-told-me-to-
launch-a-war model – but, for the average Brit, it is still a
little scary.'[16] At least for the media, public religion is something that verges on the irrational. It is consequently far safer
to base moral values on something more rational, as Gordon
Brown has tended to do in his elevation of the Scottish
Enlightenment. Even though Adam Smith was the public
philosopher most championed during the Thatcher years,
Gordon Brown has devoted considerable energy to rehabil-
itating him for the left. Focusing on Smith's *Theory of Moral
Sentiments*, Brown read Smith in terms of his elevation of
altruism and 'prudence'.[17] This was clear from the very
beginning of his time as Chancellor. As he said on 6 May
1997, the central economic objectives of the new Government could 'only happen if we build from solid foundations
of prudent economic management and sound finance'.[18] In
a recent book on Adam Smith, Iain McLean has noted the
similarities between Brown and Smith in this understanding
of prudence, which he sees as a kind of latent Presbyt-
erianism: 'once a Presbyterian, always a Presbyterian, even if
you reject the doctrines of the Church of Scotland ... Both
the eminent sons of Kirkcaldy,' he goes on, 'are puritanical
about ostentation in clothes or tastes. "Prudence" is the
favourite word of both.'[19] This, it must be said, is a very long
way from the religion of the Westminster Confession.

On not doing God: Tony Blair

In saying very little about his personal faith commitments, Gordon Brown was following in the path set by his predecessor. Tony Blair had shown a similar reluctance to speak openly of his faith – he was known as a Christian, and regularly attended churches, but he said remarkably little about how he understood Christianity or his personal commitments. His biographer, Anthony Seldon, commented that 'he's a profoundly religious figure. Religion brought him into politics in the first place, not reading Labour Party history.'[20] And it came as little surprise that in December 2007, after he had resigned as Prime Minister, he converted to the Roman Catholicism of his wife, Cherie Booth, and his children. In the BBC documentary made about his years in power broadcast in November 2007, Blair said that his faith was 'hugely important'. 'There is no point in me denying it,' he went on, 'I happen to have religious conviction. I don't actually think there is anything wrong in having religious conviction – on the contrary, I think it is a strength for people.' Nevertheless, during his years in power he had hardly ever spoken of his conviction, for fear of being labelled 'a nutter'. Public religion was evidently a sign of insanity.

The British embarrassment about speaking about religion had become obvious to Tony Blair on a number of occasions during his time in office. There had been something of an outcry when he had commented in a television interview with Michael Parkinson on 4 March 2006 in reply to a question about how he would look back on his intervention in Iraq. The interview had begun with a discussion about his political and personal development. 'Was there one moment,' Parkinson asked, 'was there a book, was there a meeting with somebody, which changed you, which changed your perspective?' Blair replied that there 'were people at university who got me in to politics, I kind of got in to religion and politics at the same time in a way.' Parkinson pressed Blair further about how this religion had manifested itself during his time as Prime Minister: 'Does it still inform your view of politics and of the world?' Blair replied: 'Well I think if you have a religious belief it does, but it's probably best not to take it too far.' Parkinson pressed him, asking Blair directly about how his religion had affected the decision to go to war: 'The only way you can take a decision like that,' he replied, 'is to try to do the right thing according to your conscience ... I think if you have faith about these things, then you realise that that judgement is made by other people ... and if you believe in God, it's made by God as well.' When Parkinson asked whether he prayed, Blair replied:

> I don't want to go into that ... you struggle with your own conscience about it ... in the end, you do what you think is the right thing ... That decision has to be taken and has to be lived with, and in the end there is a judgement that, well, I think if you have faith about these things then you realise that judgement is made by other people, and also by ... I mean by other people, by, if you believe in God, it's made by God as well and that judgement in the end has to be, you know, you do your ... The only way you can take a decision like that is to try to do the right thing according to your conscience, and for the rest of it you leave it, as I say, to the judgement that history will make.

Parkinson again asked: 'So you would pray to God when you make a decision like that?' Again Blair was evasive in his reply. This modest debate about faith-based politics on a prime-time chat show led to a degree of hysteria in the press. This included an extraordinary and highly tasteless comparison between Blair and the Yorkshire Ripper (who had claimed to hear voices from God) by Brian Reade in the *Daily Mirror*.[21] The style of reporting on ITN News provoked Blair to legal action.[22]

What this revealed was that speaking about God in public was a high-risk strategy: as portrayed in the media, religion evidently seriously clouded judgement and was best left out of politics. Blair's advisers had realised this earlier on in his time as Prime Minister. His chief spin-doctor, Alastair Campbell, famously intervened in 2003 during an interview on board an aeroplane between Blair and the columnist David Margolick for a profile in *Vanity Fair* for Blair's fiftieth birthday. When Margolick asked Blair about his faith, Campbell intervened: 'Is he on God? We don't do God. I'm sorry, we don't do God.' Blair had been effectively silenced about speaking of his faith since a lengthy article in the *Daily Telegraph* in 1996 when he had said, 'I can't stand politicians who wear God on their sleeves.'[23] By 2003, it was even claimed that Blair's spin-doctors had intervened to prevent him ending his message at the outbreak of hostilities with Iraq with the seemingly innocuous, 'God bless you.'[24]

Shortly beforehand, in February 2003, Blair was interviewed by Jeremy Paxman for a special edition of the BBC's *Newsnight* from the North-East before a live audience. The grand inquisitor asked the Prime Minister whether the fact that both he and George Bush were Christians helped them 'perceive what is good and what is evil'. He then went on to ask: 'You don't pray together for example?' Blair replied emphatically and with a slight hint of a snigger: 'No, we don't pray together Jeremy, no.' Blair then smiled, which led Paxman to ask: 'Why do you smile?' Blair responded: 'Because – why do you ask me the question?' Paxman answered: 'Because I'm trying to find out how you feel about it.' Blair concluded the encounter with a single word: 'Possibly', obviously thinking that Paxman was deliberately trying to label him as a religious fanatic.[25]

Religion was clearly something that should not be allowed to colour political judgement.

It was only after Blair had left office that he was able to talk more openly about his faith. In the BBC documentary, *The Blair Years*, Alastair Campbell commented that, contrary to his earlier outburst, Blair

> does do God in quite a big way … I think his close circle always understood that there was a part of him that was really, really important, just in the logistical level, wherever you were in the world on a Sunday you had to find a church. As it were, on that kind of spiritual level it did inform a lot of what he talked about, what he read … what he felt was important.

Similarly Peter Mandelson, one of the architects of the New Labour landslide, said that Blair was 'not an exhibitionist when it comes to religion but deep inside him it is very, very important. This is a man who takes a Bible with him wherever he goes and last thing at night he will read from the Bible.' In the documentary Blair was fairly candid about his faith:

> You know if I am honest about it, yes of course it was hugely important. You know you can't have a religious faith and it be an insignificant aspect because it's, it's profound about you and about you as a human being … As I always say there is no point in me denying it, I happen to have religious conviction, I don't actually think there is anything wrong in having religious conviction – on the contrary I think it is a strength for people.

Asked about Alastair Campbell's refusal to allow discussion of faith, Blair replied that it was not because he was opposed to faith, 'but because you always get into trouble talking about it. So anyway here we are talking about it.' Campbell agreed: 'I just always worry in Britain the public

are a bit wary of politicians who go on about God.' Blair
expanded on the same theme:

> It's difficult if you talk about religious faith in our
> political system. I mean if you are in the American
> political system or others then you can talk about
> religious faith and people say 'yes, that's fair enough'
> and it is something they respond to quite naturally ...
> You talk about it in our system and frankly people do
> think you're a nutter. I mean they sort of, you know
> you maybe go off and sit in the corner and you
> know commune with, with the man upstairs and then
> come back and say right I've been told the answer and
> that's it.

This passage unwittingly says a great deal about the complexity of relating religion to public policy in the British
system. Religion is perceived as somehow irrational and
clouding judgement. Since it is regarded as dealing in rights
and wrongs and blacks and whites, it would make the
complexities and shades of grey of *Realpolitik* particularly
problematic. A politician who prays – as Blair's telling smile
to Paxman revealed – was already likely to be seen as com-
muning with the fairies, and certainly not fit for public
office. So secularised had Britain become that being publicly religious was effectively a sign of unsound mind,
although there were few who criticised Blair for attending
church. Going to church was an acceptable practice provided that Christianity was not explicitly spoken of anywhere
else.

Since leaving office, Tony Blair has devoted considerable energy and commitment to promoting dialogue
between the religions. Indeed, he claims that 'the issue of
religious faith will be of the same significance to the 21st
Century as political ideology was to the 20th Century'.[26]
He has set up the Tony Blair Faith Foundation, contribut-
ing a lecture on 'Faith and Globalisation' to the Westminster

Cathedral Series in April 2008. He tackled the question of 'doing God' head on, suggesting that there were five reasons why Alastair Campbell had made his famous comment:

> First, you may be considered weird. Normal people aren't supposed to 'do God'. Second, there is an assumption that before you take a decision, you engage in some slightly cultish interaction with your religion – 'So, God, tell me what you think of City Academies or Health Service Reform or nuclear power' – i.e. people assume that your religion makes you act, as a leader, at the promptings of an inscrutable deity, free from reason rather than in accordance with it.
>
> Third, you want to impose your religious faith on others.
>
> Fourth, you are pretending to be better than the next person.
>
> And finally and worst of all, that you are somehow messianically trying to co-opt God to bestow a divine legitimacy on your politics.[27]

All this indicated that religion was regarded by many as something 'divisive, irrational and harmful'. However, it could also present a very different picture, what he called 'enacted love of neighbour'. He concluded:

> If people of different faiths can co-exist happily, in mutual respect and solidarity, so can our world. And if faith takes its proper place in our lives, then we can live with a purpose beyond ourselves alone, supporting humanity on its journey to fulfilment.

It was this picture that he was hoping to present to the world through his forthcoming lectures at Yale University. Faith could be a positive force for good and integration.

The Scottish social historian Callum Brown has written perceptively about the situation facing politicians who profess faith in contemporary Britain:

Most Britons left their culture of Christian faith over the last forty years, without on the whole much rancour or bitterness. They have no particular cause today to rise in austere protest against those who, like Blair, might still profess faith. Their evacuation of this territory imparts to those who still occupy it, like Blair, an awareness that it can't be pushed too far. There would be a cultural incomprehension if it were … In the United States, Bush and every president before him has been able to proclaim the role of God in their lives as a badge of office. But if the culture of Christianity is still dominant there, in Britain – as indeed (and distinctively) in most of Europe – the culture of a dominant faith is now long gone. The prospect of it ever returning at present lacks any significant evidence. In that situation, no politician dare speak too much of the role of God in government. For the sake of the seemingly contented secular culture of the vast majority, the professing rhetoric of the astute faith politician best not to be taken too far.[28]

Callum Brown, it seems to me, is accurate in his estimation of the possibilities for faith-politicians in Britain. And it is undeniable that, despite the rhetoric of some religious people and church leaders, Britain is a highly secularised society.[29] There is something not quite acceptable about public declarations of faith as anything more than a vague synonym for a set of universal human values – those who venture into the forbidden territory are at the very least liable to experience ridicule.

Britain: A secular country

The problems faced by politicians who profess faith reveal the extraordinary extent to which Britain is to all intents and purposes a secular society. Although statistics about religious affiliation are never easy to interpret, it is difficult to read the data in any other way than as evidence of a significant detachment from religion among most of the population. However, this is not immediately apparent from the national census of 2001, which, for the first time, asked a question about religious affiliation. Although this question provoked some criticism, nearly three-quarters of the population were nevertheless prepared to label themselves as Christian, and a further 6 per cent or so claimed allegiance to other religions (including Jedi). The question asked was simply: 'What is your religion?' The detailed numbers were as follows:[30]

	Total population		**Non-Christian religious population**
	(Numbers)	(Percentages)	(Percentages)
Christian	41,014,811	71.8	
Muslim	1,588,890	2.8	51.9
Hindu	558,342	1.0	18.3
Sikh	336,179	0.6	11.0
Jewish	267,373	0.5	8.7
Buddhist	149,157	0.3	4.9
Any other religion	159,167	0.3	5.2
All non-Christian religious population	3,059,108	5.4	100.0
No religion	8,596,488	15.1	
Religion not stated	4,433,520	7.8	
All population	57,103,927	100.0	

Population of Great Britain: by religion, April 2001

The seemingly high number of Christians seems to counter the claims of secularisation theorists. It may, however, be simply explained in terms of the question which had been asked. There was no mention of affiliation to a church or membership of a group, which means that people may simply have been forced to think about religious identity in negative terms – they knew they were not Muslim or Hindu and were therefore Christian. Besides, precisely what would be meant by 'belonging' to a Christian institution like the Church of England is difficult to interpret. It is open to all comers and regards all people as potentially its 'members' in that they have the right to make use of its services: every corner of England is covered by a territorial parish system. Allegiance is so loose that membership is a fairly meaningless term – particularly in the countryside many people will regard the local parish church as 'their' church even though they have never attended a service.

A number of more recent surveys have found significantly lower numbers of people calling themselves Christian than the 2001 national census. In a report commissioned by the Evangelical mission agency Tearfund,[31] which was based on a survey of 7,000 adults, the question was asked: 'Do you regard yourself as belonging to any particular religion?' This was evidently a more searching question than that asked in the census. In response, about 53 per cent of the population claimed to 'belong' in some sense to Christianity (about 26.2 million adults), and about a further 6 per cent to other religions (about 3.2 million). This number was broadly similar to a number of other reports, including the Government's British Social Attitudes Survey: 15 per cent of adults attended church at least once a month (7.6 million), with a further 3 per cent (1.6 million) going at least 6 times per year. Another 7 per cent (3.4 million) attended at least once a year. Again, numbers were broadly in line with the 2005 English Religious Census conducted by Christian Research on 8 May 2005, which estimated that there were 3,166,200 adults and children in church in England on that day or about 6.3 per cent of the population.[32]

The Tearfund survey found that 28 per cent of adults (13.7 million) claimed to have attended church at some time in the past but were unlikely to do so again (the 'dechurched'). A further 32 per cent of adults (15.6 million) had never been to church in their life, except for weddings, baptisms or funerals (the 'unchurched'). The conclusions which were drawn from the Tearfund survey were that about two-thirds of UK adults are 'secular in that they have no connection with church at present. The vast majority of these – 29.3 million – are "closed" to attending church in future (equivalent to 60 per cent of all adults).'[33] This is striking evidence for the loss of significant Christianity from the majority of the adult population of Britain.

The numbers attending the mainline churches have continued to drop rapidly. The two largest denominations have fallen to a weekly attendance of well below a million. The 2006 UK Church Survey estimated that there were 861,800 Roman Catholics attending church weekly compared with 852,500 Anglicans. The larger number of Catholics was accounted for by the significant numbers of new immigrants from Poland and other countries with far higher levels of religious practice. Participation in religion is a key factor of ethnic identity, particular among immigrant populations. Regular churchgoing is also much higher among adults of black ethnic origin, and stands at over three times that of white adults. The 2005 UK Church Survey[34] found that about 10 cent of all churchgoers were black, with 44 per cent in inner London.

Britain, it should be noted, is not significantly different from other European countries. The European Social Survey of 2002 found that about 18.6 per cent of UK adults attended religious services at least once a month, which was broadly similar to Germany, the Netherlands, Belgium and

Hungary, and higher than in France and Denmark.[35] Some other countries, most notably Poland, have retained much higher levels of religious practice, although the latest evidence suggests that they are beginning to experience a steep decline in churchgoing.

While it is extremely difficult to estimate attendances in the past, given the lack of reliable statistics, it has been variously suggested that in 1851, at the time of the Census of Religious Worship, church attendance was between 30–35 per cent[36] and 61.5–65.1 per cent.[37] Even if this lower figure is accepted, this still means that there has been an enormous decline in the numbers of active churchgoers. Church membership in 1900 stood at approximately 27 per cent of the population compared to about 10 per cent in 2000.[38] Robin Gill, who has worked on churchgoing in the outer London suburb of Bromley, formerly in Kent, estimated that in 1903 about 31 per cent of the population was in church compared to about 10.5 per cent in 1993.[39] While all these figures are open to question, and the precise timings of decline have been the subject of much recent scholarly debate (between, for instance, Callum Brown[40] and Hugh McLeod),[41] the evidence is incontrovertible. Something like two-thirds of the people of Great Britain have little if any attachment to a faith community. There is no evidence that attachment to new religions or 'holistic spirituality' is likely to make up for the decline of Christianity.[42] Some see the future of religious affiliation as increasingly likely to become de-institutionalised, so that 'being religious' will be little different from taking part in some sort of alliance for social justice (like Fair Trade or climate change).[43] For the most part, then, religion is either private or non-existent, and Britain is a secular society. Given this dominant framework of secularism, the resurgence of public religion – especially Islam – is difficult to accommodate within the current political structures which are premised on a secularised world-view. As Tariq Modood writes: 'The emergence of Muslim political agency has thrown multiculturalism into theoretical and practical disarray.'[44] This clash of cultures has led to significant levels of conflict across Europe.

The clash of the religious with the secular: the need for pluralism

As José Casanova suggested in his ground-breaking book on public religion,[45] modern societies are experiencing what he has called a 'deprivatisation' of religion. Across Europe there has been a frequent clash between the 'secular' and the religious, most obviously in the headscarves controversy (the *affaire de foulard*) in French state schools.[46] How the state deals with the regulation of 'minority' religions has meant an significant politicisation of religion, not simply in France, even if its secular tradition of *laïcité* has made the conflicts rather more heated. The 'poorly framed' French law against symbols and clothing 'through which they exhibit conspicuously a religious affiliation,' writes one commentator, 'stigmatises a small section of the population as un-French in a manner reminiscent of the Dreyfus Affair: it suggests the fundamental inability of large sections of the French media and government to adapt to the varied and complex cultural framework set in the processes of globalisation.'[47] While in itself the veil may have little significance in Islam and may well be relatively modern, it can quickly become a boundary marker, an expression of embodied spirituality among those occupying a marginal position. The veil becomes a symbol of what has been called the 'frontier body'.[48] It deliberately marks out 'difference' rather than commonness and thus presents a challenge to the uniformity of the state. In response, the state (or even the public corporation like British Airways) is forced to eliminate the symbol through enforced secularism against any form of public religious expression. This will obviously mean that religion will be treated as a private matter. In such cases, however, such an approach can easily lead to further marginalisation, retrenchment, and even radicalisation among minorities.[49]

The alternative to such secularism is to engage seriously with pluralism. In general British multi-cultural policy has moved in this direction, although frequently it has maintained a covert secularism which has tended to regard religion and cultural identity as something essentially private. Increasingly public (and political) expressions of religious and cultural identity, however, mean that what Tariq Modood calls an 'active state policy of multiculturalism' which recognises the country as a 'legitimate and irreducible plurality' or 'community of communities' will become crucial.[50] I finished *Blair's Britain* with a similar call for pluralism. As I will show in the next chapter, it seems to me that implicit in much recent Government thinking has been a general acceptance of the need for pluralism: the idea of a public ethnic and religious identity as the primary focus for belonging, especially among the marginalised, has been accepted as something of a commonplace. Similarly, the importance of the 'community' and 'neighbourhood' as a place for making policy and taking decisions has been widely recognised. Yet at the same time there are powerful forces which make pluralism difficult to put into practice. Centralised decision-making and economic prudence implemented through target-driven managerialism continue to threaten the development of a pluralist society. This centralism has led to the stifling of participatory democracy at the local level.

More importantly, however, – and this is something I scarcely addressed in *Blair's Britain* – is the issue of shared identity between the different groups. What are the values of, for example, 'Britishness' which bind people of different communities and groups together? Gordon Brown has sensed something of the need for shared values in many of his speeches both before and after his appointment as Prime Minister, but there is a vagueness and somewhat nostalgic nationalism in many of his utterances. Nevertheless the limits of pluralism need to be defined to ensure that freedoms are protected. As Modood writes:

> the plural state, unlike the liberal state, is able to offer an emotional identity with the whole to counterbalance the emotional loyalties to ethnic and religious communities, which should prevent the fragmentation of society into narrow, selfish communalisms, while the presence of these strong community identities will be an effective check against monocultural statism.[51]

This is something that requires neither the implementation of a state-directed policy of secularism and neutrality, nor a set of traditional 'British' or 'English' values, but a rather more modest self-critical attitude from both the state and its constituent communities, which needs to be upheld by law. In what I propose through the course of this book, especially in the final chapter, this system of checks and balances will be a constant process rather than an achievement – politics will therefore be a process of perpetual dialogue rather than premature foreclosure.

CHAPTER TWO

Building Community

In *Blair's Britain* I spent a fair bit of time looking at how the word 'community' was used in the rhetoric and policy initiatives of New Labour and the subsequent Labour Government.[1] I also took account of how similar 'Third Way' thinking with its emphasis on 'community' had been used in government policy in both South Africa and Germany. On a careful reading it turned out that community was a very vague term indeed which, though frequently used, was short on content. The basic gist of the Government rhetoric was that communities were good things, and provided a far better structure for human society than simply lots of isolated individuals struggling incoherently to live together. Communities were therefore to be encouraged – they were to provide the building blocks for a more pluralist society than was possible for either the individualism of secular liberalism or the monochrome identity of state socialism. This sort of thinking has continued in Government thinking, and has provided the basis for the multicultural policy of recent years, which has focused on building and strengthening sustainable cultural communities at the local level, which are distinct from the 'national' community.

At the same time there has been a competing rhetoric which has been particularly pronounced in Gordon Brown's speeches and writings. This has concentrated on the idea of shared 'British' values, which undergird the diversities of the different communities making up the modern United Kingdom. There are tensions between these two sets of policies – one tends towards a locally based pluralism established on the recognition of difference between communities and with only a minimal emphasis on 'national' identity, while the other has stressed 'citizenship' and common identity in the freedoms of the British constitution. Both may be necessary, but the precise balance is unclear in Government thinking. Given the long history of strong and centralised executive power, however, those who wish to establish devolved decision-making, especially in England, will have to work particularly hard. Behind the different and competing rhetorical strategies are real tensions between national and local government. This chapter outlines the development of what has been called the 'new localism' as this has affected recent Government policy. In the next chapter I go on to discuss what I have chosen to call the 'old nationalism' and the politics of Britishness. These different conceptions of community provide the backdrop for Chapter 4, which offers a detailed analysis of the place of the state in 'community cohesion' and its social and political implications.

Social capital

The elevation of the local community at the expense of the national is hardly a novel idea. It is something that has found champions among so-called 'communitarian' thinkers on both the left and right of the political spectrum.[2] One factor that has been particularly influential in the most recent thinking, especially in the emphasis on devolution to the local community, derives from a set of ideas which have been called 'social capital' (or sometimes, in Pierre Bourdieu's less positive language, 'cultural capital').[3] Writing about social capital in his influential *Bowling Alone*, Robert Putnam claimed straightforwardly and directly that those who live together in a 'durable network' or 'connective tissue' of relationships improve their life chances and productivity. In short, he wrote, 'our lives are made more productive by social ties'.[4] On the basis of this economic analogy he develops a relatively simple thesis. Social capital has declined and needs to be reconstructed for the healthy functioning of society. Writing about his own American context, he traces the decline in community activity over the past 30 years or so. Whereas earlier in the twentieth century there had been a deep engagement in the life of communities which was manifested in a whole range of group activities, in recent years things had changed beyond recognition. 'Silently, without warning', he wrote, 'that tide reversed and we were overtaken by a treacherous rip current. Without at first noticing, we have been pulled apart from one another and from our communities over the last third of the century.'[5] According to Putnam, the evidence for this collapse of social capital was that voluntary organisations and other agents of community had been in significant decline. The consequence of this loss of participation in social activities was huge shifts in the levels of 'social capital',[6] which he equated with what he called 'connections among individuals'. He sees these connections in terms of the

> social networks and the norm of reciprocity and trustworthiness that arise from them. In that sense, social capital is closely related to what some have called 'civic virtue.' The difference is that 'social capital' calls attention to the fact that civic virtue is most powerful when embedded in a dense network of reciprocal social relations. A society of many virtuous but isolated individuals is not necessarily rich in social capital.[7]

The knock-on effects of this decline in social capital would be the loss of this civic virtue, which he understood as those invisible forces which helped societies to cohere through altruistic and community-focused activity. Consequently, in what he regards as something of a vicious circle, Putnam sees the decline of social capital as both the cause and effect of contemporary social problems.[8] He concludes with a plea for what he calls

> an era of civic inventiveness to create a renewed set of institutions and channels for a reinvigorated civic life that will fit the way we have come to live. Our challenge now is to reinvent the twenty-first century equivalent of the Boy Scouts or the settlement house or the playground.[9]

Policies aimed at revitalising local communities can be understood as part of this 'civic inventiveness', and required a significant level of investment in social capital. As communities were bonded together through face-to-face corporate activities, so they became more cohesive, and thereby better able to bridge the distances with other communities.[10] Properly altruistic communities would not then tend to define themselves over and against other communities engaged in the wider network of society.

Many other social and political commentators have spoken of the decline in 'social capital' as one of the main problems of recent years. While obviously related to a broader set of long-term sociological issues of urbanisation and the uprooting of people from traditional patterns of community life resulting from the division of labour, some have seen the 1980s and 1990s as the pinnacle of the decline in social capital. For some, society appeared to be being rebuilt on unbounded individualism and survival of the fittest. This has occasionally led some to make some unguarded apocalyptic claims about what was happening to Britain. In a rather overstated essay with lots of italics, for instance, the Polish cultural theorist and commentator, Zygmunt Bauman has written that 'every single measure of the Thatcher/Blair programme [has contributed] to the *progressive decomposition and crumbling of social bonds and communal cohesion*'.[11] New policies to overcome what he calls 'wilting solidarity' thus become crucial for the good functioning of democracy and society, as people are once again encouraged to participate as actors in the 'social state'.[12] For the time being, however, all that remains is a 'pulverised' society of 'solitary individuals':

> Among many bright ideas for which Margaret Thatcher will be remembered was her discovery of the non-existence of society ... 'There is no such thing as "society" ... There are only individuals and families' – she said. But Tony Blair may well yet be remembered for making that figment of Thatcher's imagination into a fairly precise description of the real world, as seen from the *inside* of its inhabitants' experience.[13]

The argument runs that unbridled consumerism in all walks of life, together with the progressive dismantling of the social state and local democracy and accountability, have led to unprecedentedly low levels of social capital. It is hardly surprising that among many commentators and theorists – not to mention theologians – there is something of a longing for small-scale communities as the panacea for the failures of both big government and the excesses of Thatcherite (and, if one believes Bauman, Blairite) individualism. It must be said, however, that much New Labour language has sought to promote quite the opposite of unbridled individualism: fostering cohesive communities and restoring social capital have been high on the political agenda for the past 11 years and they show no sign of disappearing.

Community and society

This sort of thinking on the importance of community is, of course, far from new. At least historically the goals and tasks of much recent Government policy as well as the clamours for strong community in many other quarters resemble those of sociology, at least in the early years of its existence as an independent discipline at the turn of the twentieth century. For most early sociologists, sociology was not simply about impartial investigation of society, but also – and far more importantly – about social improvement and the amelioration of the appalling living conditions which were side-effects of modernisation. It often sought to intro-duce 'scientific' methods of social engineering for the promotion of what it frequently called community – at its beginning most sociology was a long way from being a value-neutral discipline undertaken by social scientists (whatever the claims made by some, like Auguste Comte, who regarded it as a positive science). This task of social improvement required a set of myths, which were usually centred on the over-arching historical myth of a pre-modern form of social order called 'community' which was associated with villages, which were contrasted with the far less tightly knit and more anonymous structures of modern industrial society.[14] What was important in understanding community was that it was something which depended on face-to-face contact and it was measured in terms of the density and frequency of human contact. Hardly surprising-ly, communities were also deeply religious, since all people shared the same patterns of beliefs and all participated in the same rites of passage.[15] Community could be glimpsed in its purest form in the stable pre-modern communities of the past where people did not move around much, where they worked at home or in the fields, and where everybody knew everybody else.[16]

In this understanding of social organisation, the influence of one of the first German sociologists, Ferdinand Tönnies, cannot be overestimated. Tönnies differentiated between what he regarded as the two key forms of social organisation, loosely translated as 'community' (*Gemeinschaft*) and 'society' (*Gesellschaft*). 'Being together,' he wrote,

> is the vegetative heart and soul of Community (*Gemeinschaft*) – the very existence of *Gemeinschaft* rests in the consciousness of belonging together and the affirmation of the condition of mutual dependence which is posed by that affirmation. Living together may be called the animal soul of *Gemeinschaft*; for it is the condition of its active life, of a shared feeling of pleasure and pain, of a shared enjoyment of the commonly possessed goods, by which one is surrounded, and by the cooperation in teamwork as well as in divided labour. Working together may be conceived of as the rational or human soul of *Gemeinschaft*. It is a higher, more conscious cooperation in the unity of spirit and purpose, including, therefore, a striving for common or shared ideals, as invisible goods that are knowable only to thought. Regarding being together it is descent (blood), regarding living together it is soil (land), regarding working together it is occupation (*Beruf*) that is the substance, as it were, by which the wills of men, which otherwise are far apart from and even antagonistic to each other, are essentially united.[17]

The concept of community, as this reveals, is deeply rooted in kinship as well as in the historical myths of 'blood' and 'soil'. On this model, community 'cohesion' is dependent on a shared ethnicity and occupation of a piece of land.

A similar set of ideas was displayed in England by a number of important Victorian thinkers, perhaps most notably the constitutional historian, Edward Freeman.

Waxing lyrical about the origins of English freedom, he wrote of its survival in its purest form only in the communities of Switzerland: 'Year by year, on certain spots among the dales and mountainsides of Switzerland [one can look] face to face on freedom in its purest and most ancient form.'[18] In distinction, modern societies were quite different. Crucially, they had lost this sense of connectedness with place and their unity established on common beliefs and pursuits. For many sociologists and historians – including most notably Émile Durkheim, who was deeply influenced by Tönnies – society needed to be reinvigorated through the conscious re-creation of the values of community (or what he called 'organic solidarity'). In his great book, *The Division of Labour in Society*, Durkheim sought to establish a new form of small-scale community founded on choice and co-operation rather than tradition and birthright.[19] In Durkheim and many others there is inevitably a romanticism and an element of wishful thinking – which was also present in many Victorian historians – which they felt might provide a solution to the perceived breakdown of modern society. Indeed, there is a sense of nostalgic melancholia running through much sociological and historical thought. Many later nineteenth-century figures could even be described as 'Gothic sociologists'.[20] As Durkheim wrote at the end of *The Elementary Forms of the Religious Life*:

> this state of uncertainty and bewildered turmoil cannot last forever. A day will come when our societies will again know those times of creative effervescence in which new ideas will spring up and new formulae will be discovered to serve for a while as a guide to humanity.[21]

For Durkheim, as for many others, there was a desire for something new which would re-create the spark of the old world which had been energised by religion and other ways of affirming community identity. It seems to me that there is a similar longing in much of the recent thought which has found its way into British Government policy: against the disintegrating effects of modern society there seems to be a clamour to return to something simpler.

Indeed, it is not implausible to see politicians as the new sociologists, and to read the history of the relationship between sociology and politics as one of exchange and replacement. And, given the relationship between sociology and theology, which had to some extent been one of exchange and replacement, politicians may in a sense be heirs of the religious tradition of community-formation – increased 'social capital' may be understood as a kind of secularised ecclesiology. Thus, perhaps ironically, as sociology became less involved with amelioration and social reconstruction and more concerned with objective social analysis, so the role of government expanded to embrace the ameliorative (and romantic) tasks of sociology which were to be achieved through community-formation. Sociologists of secularisation have tended to see the state authorities as usurping the role of the churches in caring for the poor and sick. This meant that churches suffered from a loss of role and status.[22] This transformation, however, is equally true of sociology, which lost its ameliorative soul to politics. Political rhetoric adopted many of the same myths of the 'common vision' of community which had once guided both sociologists and historians, and many politicians saw their brief as resting in the re-creation of local communities bound together by common purpose. If this is the case then politics is ultimately the grandchild of religion.

The new Tuscans

It may even be true that the clamour for community by so many recent politicians amounts to an unconscious re-creation of a historic myth, something like a new version of the old myth of the free village community of Anglo-Saxon times upholding the ancient Teutonic freedoms.[23] It is not a long journey from Freeman and other great Victorian historians like William Stubbs to Ruth Kelly's version of the national myth based on what she called 'building up a shared sense of purpose and belonging' in a speech given to the Commission for Racial Equality in November 2006.[24] There is some connection, it seems to me, between the sociological and historical understanding of community and the sort of rhetoric used in recent Government policies. There is a longing for some sort of British identity which will be located first and foremost not in the national state, but in the local community with its happy festivities and vibrant and colourful street life. Despite the weather, Tessa Jowell, when Secretary of State for Culture, thought Britain would be transformed into a relaxed European country with a peaceful café culture rather than the binge drinking of city centres. Longer pub opening hours would mark the beginning of this transformation in such unlikely places as Gateshead.[25]

The presence of people like Tessa Jowell in the Cabinet perhaps reveals something of the source of this sort of policy. The impact of Tuscan urban life on the politics of New Labour should never be underestimated. As became clear in the corruption allegations surrounding her estranged husband, David Mills in 2007, Jowell had the use of a villa in Tuscany.[26] Siena's *palio* with its colourful contests between the 17 *contrade*, which happens in the height of the holiday season, displays a strong sense of local identity and solidarity. A week later, for the festival of the Assumption, the city-dwellers spend their time organising attractive parades through the streets. While this might be to overstate things slightly, one cannot help thinking that perhaps in the back of the minds of the middle-class policy makers who have seen these sorts of jollifications is the thought: 'If only we could do those sorts of things in Britain.' Frank Dobson, a previous Secretary of State for Health, was perhaps more realistic about building Tuscany in Britain: 'The English – maybe the British – have been binge drinkers since time immemorial. I don't think we'll turn into Tuscany just because the hours have changed.'[27]

A Department for Communities

This sociological and historical thinking provides something of the background to the revival of talk about communities in recent British politics, particularly about how local communities should be governed and how the different levels of government relate to one another. There has been a significant emphasis on shifting power to local communities, which forms part of what has been referred to as 'the new localism', which amounts to a contract or partnership between local organisations, local government and national Government 'to support the delivery of local objectives and national targets'.[28] This has been a central focus of policy across several Government departments in recent years.[29] Indeed, since I published *Blair's Britain* in early 2005, where I devoted a chapter to 'community' as it had been used by New Labour, British Government thinking on community has moved on remarkably quickly. The most important development has undoubtedly been the mutation of the Office of the Deputy Prime Minister into the Department for Communities and Local Government, which took place on 5 May 2006. This emerged after John Prescott's sexual and financial misdemeanours which led to his removal from nearly all of his ministerial responsibilities even before the accession of Gordon Brown. Initially the new department was headed up by Ruth Kelly who set the policy objectives and produced the first White Paper. In the reshuffle of 28 June 2007, following the appointment of the new Prime Minister, she was replaced by

Hazel Blears, who had a background in local politics in Salford.

Ruth Kelly's vision as first Secretary of State, which she offered shortly after her appointment, was to create a Department which is on the

> side of people who want to make a difference, where everyone has the opportunity to fulfil their potential and to build a stake in society for them and their families. We want strong, cohesive communities in which people feel comfortable and proud to live, with a vibrant civic culture and strong local economy.[30]

Here there is strategic use of the terms 'community' and 'society', along with the idea of 'cohesion' (which I will discuss in more detail in Chapter 4). 'Society' is a social unit in which people who want to make a difference build a stake, and 'community' is a social group which should be strong and cohesive and where people feel both comfortable and proud to live. The core of the departmental ethos is thus founded on the virtues of wanting to make a difference through membership of a community, as well as pride in place. There are obvious resonances with the sort of thinking outlined earlier in this chapter. Precisely what 'vibrant civic culture' might look like was not spelt out. This policy has been continued by Hazel Blears. In her statement on taking office she pledged herself

> to create stable and safe communities, thriving neighbourhoods and affordable homes. I have always championed local communities, and sought to give local people more influence and control over their lives. I pledge today to carry on the work to make our communities stronger, safer and great to live in.[31]

Blears seemed to be working within a favourable political climate as she continued to follow the pattern set by her predecessor in what seemed the very laudable and uncontroversial departmental brief. This will be discussed further in Chapter 4.

Through the Department for Communities and Local Government, the British Government clearly sees itself as having a role in the promotion of strong local communities, principally through partnership with local government and other agencies including those from the voluntary or 'Third Sector' (or what it rather imprecisely calls in its mission statement 'community organisations and communities themselves').[32] Much of the rhetoric in speeches and policy documents emanating from the Department has focused on the revival of local autonomy and decision-making at the lowest possible level. The Government's principal goals for communities were spelled out at length and in great detail in the White Paper, *Strong and Prosperous Communities*, published in October 2006.[33] This document began with individuals and families but soon moved to communities. It claimed that the Government was 'on the side of individuals and families who want to make a difference, both to their own lives and to the communities in which they live'. This process of making a difference, it claimed, had radical policy implications for the governance of Britain. It required 'revitalised local authorities', and at the same time, a reduction in 'the amount of top-down control from central government'. Given the target-driven and highly directive policy of 'constrained discretion',[34] which had dominated the Blair years, especially under the influence of the Chancellor of the Exchequer, Gordon Brown (and which will be discussed in more detail in the next chapter), this would require a complete change of direction of Government policy.

However, the influence of the all-pervasive reach of Government target-setting meant that it was hardly surprising that a great deal of the centralising agenda of the Blair years remained in the document. This was particularly obvious in those sections which emphasised the consumption of services. People, the White Paper claimed, 'want choice over the services they receive, influence over those who provide them, and higher service standards'. Unwittingly perhaps, the language here continues to be shaped by an understanding of local communities and authorities as providers of services to (passive) consumers, who have little ability or power to shape the services themselves. Despite the rhetoric of decentralisation, the centralism of Government-imposed targets for 'service standards' still dominated the shape of the policy presented in the White Paper. As part of what was fundamentally a centrally-directed policy of decentralisation, local authorities would be required to set up a 'Sustainable Community Strategy' with about 35 (nationally set) priorities tailored to local needs. These would be based on 'about 200 outcome-based indicators, covering important national priorities'. In turn there would also be a delivery plan known as a 'Local Area Agreement', which would have to be ratified with central Government. The new localism was anything but locally determined but had to be agreed with some form of Orwellian bureaucracy: there are obvious tensions here between the central direction of local policy and initiatives aimed at devolving power to communities. These will be further highlighted in the next chapter.

At other times, however, the White Paper was far more radical in its calls for devolution of power to the local level. People were to be able to 'demand an answer to their questions' through a new 'Community Call for Action'. There were to be measures to promote increased community ownership and management of local facilities and assets. There was also a call for the creation of what the document dubbed as 'Quality Parish Councils', where councillors would speak out on local issues and become champions of their 'local communities'. Greater power was also to be devolved to cities and regions, although it was not spelt out precisely how this would work. Stronger local leadership would be promoted, the White Paper continued, since communities would need 'strategic leadership'. Finally, the overarching goal of the policy on communities was summarised thus: 'stronger local leadership, greater resident participation in decisions and an enhanced role for community groups, can all help local areas to promote community cohesion'. In this related area of community cohesion, where different ethnic and religious communities would be encouraged to engage and share ideas with one another, a policy delivery Quango, the 'Commission on Integration and Cohesion' was to be set up. This would produce 'detailed plans on how to deliver a step change in promoting cohesion'. According to the Government's vision, local communities would become agents of certain socially-desirable goals, among them crime-reduction, the delivery of services, and the fostering of cohesion (which will be discussed in Chapter 4).

The White Paper highlights the fundamental tensions between the local and the national, and just how much things will have to change if there is to be a real empowerment of local communities. In particular, local government has been emasculated in recent years, with most of its powers reduced to the simple delivery of policies beyond its control, and with virtually no independent revenue-raising powers.[35] The sad demise of local government has been documented by Anthony King: 'the cumulative effect' of policies of successive governments, he writes, 'has been to reduce local government to a pale shadow of its former self'. Local government is effectively the subject of endless dispute where central government has 'alternately played Good Cop and Bad Cop. Bad Cop has usually won.'[36] This means that 'the upshot of the various developments' in the relationships between local and national government is that

> local government is no longer, in any meaningful
> sense, a part of the British constitution. A past part, yes.

[38]

A future part, conceivably. But a present part, no ... it has been both imprisoned and disembowelled.[37]

These tensions have continued even in the latest policy statements, which will be discussed in the next chapter. What I will argue is that there can be no meaningful revival of community and participatory democracy without significant levels of devolution. An analogy that might mean something to the Anglican churchgoer is this: disembowelling local government is like putting bishops in control of the local churches and at the same time removing the synods and parochial church councils. No wonder most of the Elizabethan bishops thought synodical government would sow the first seeds of sedition.[38]

CHAPTER THREE

Brown, Britishness and Community

'A reinvention of the way we govern'

After Gordon Brown became Prime Minister in the summer of 2007,[1] there was a renewed public commitment by the Government to policy on community, particularly to the more radical aspects which involved increased levels of devolution to local communities. The regime change gave an opportunity to rethink local democracy and even to place the issue of constitutional change, or 'letting-go' by the centre, onto the agenda.[2] As I noted at the end of the last chapter, significant devolution would have repercussions for the British constitution itself, which was acknowledged by the new Prime Minister. As Chancellor of the Exchequer, Brown had earlier outlined his thoughts in this area in his speech to the 2006 Labour Party Conference at Manchester:

> People and communities should now take power from the state and that means for the new challenges ahead

a reinvention of the way we govern: the active citizen, the empowered community, open enabling government … It is right that local councils, not Whitehall, should have more power over the things that matter to their community and from economic regeneration to public transport, the empowerment and strengthening of local councils and local communities is what we must now do … And I will also champion community ownership of local assets and so that people who want change can secure that change, community petitions to trigger action. And in that spirit of devolution I want to work with the lottery so that for even the smallest community, local budgets for local community facilities can be voted on by local people.[3]

This speech certainly signalled a change of gear, and possibly also a complete reversal from Brown in relation to local government. Coming from somebody who has so frequently been derided as 'psychologically flawed' (Andrew Rawnsley), a 'control-freak' (Charles Clarke) or a 'crypto-Stalinist' (Lord Turnbull), any support for devolution to local communities is a major concession.[4]

Hazel Blears began work as Secretary of State for Communities by expanding on these policies outlined by Gordon Brown. Shortly after her appointment, in a major speech to the Local Government Association given in July 2007,[5] she began by claiming that her 'whole political approach, fashioned on the streets and estates of Salford, is anchored in localism and devolution'. She called for the active involvement of local people in decision-making since, as she put it, 'there's more common sense on the average street or estate than in all of the think tanks and seminars put together'. 'Devolving power from Whitehall to the Town Hall, and from the Town Hall to local communities', she went on, 'is not just the right thing to do, it's the most effective way to build places where people are proud to live, work and raise their family.' What she called 'daily democracy' was to be at the heart of the new government, which would focus on Community Cohesion or 'how we celebrate the values we all share and that help us draw strength from our diversity'. She recognised that the White Paper was overly prescriptive, and announced the reduction in the number of indicators 'from over 1,000 to around 200' (which was the number that it had in fact claimed). Somewhat inconsistently, given that they were supposed to have had their residual power transferred to local communities, local authorities would nevertheless have 'unprecedented discretion to direct funding to meet those targets'. 'I believe', she continued, 'that the biggest improvements in public services are driven not by the oversight of central government, but by local people. By communities having a chance to say what they want.' The future of the relationships between local democracy and local autonomy is far from clear.[6]

Blears also spoke of the importance of transferring public assets to communities, a proposal that had been developed at length by Barry Quirk, Chief Executive Officer of Lewisham Council and the (national) Government's Local Government Efficiency Adviser, in his report, *Making Assets Work*.[7] Ownership of community assets would create 'active citizens'. 'The greater the stake,' the report claimed, 'the greater the financial and legal responsibility the organisation takes on, but also the greater the freedom to exploit the assets' potential.'[8] A third policy objective was 'participatory budgeting', which was also referred to as the 'people's purse' or the 'community kitty'.[9] This was aimed at

> giving some of the poorest, most powerless and dispossessed people ... a stake in their future ... Giving people direct and transparent choice about how funds are allocated in their local area not only makes sure

their priorities are being met. It's a way of making them feel more able to say 'this is my street, my estate, and I'm proud of it.' Devolution right to the doorstep.

These different aspects of devolution were to be underpinned by the institutions of an accountable local democracy which would make agreements with national Government (even if some existing council powers were to be delegated further down).

In a series of speeches during her frenetic time at the Department, Blears has presented these themes of devolution and the 'new localism', stressing Brown's 'reinvention of Government', a phrase that she has repeated in virtually all her statements. In speeches about 'Confident Communities' and 'Bringing Devolution to Life' she announced that 'localism' was 'moving from the fringes of the political agenda to the very heart',[10] and that the reforms were 'bringing Government closer to people, passing power from Whitehall to the town hall and direct to local communities'.[11] This was, she claimed, the 'best way to revitalise the local roots of our democracy' and of 'making local services reflect people's needs'. She continued: 'I want to make the Department for Communities and Local Government the Department for Governing Differently.' As well as local transfer of assets and participatory budgeting, this also involved the idea of 'community anchors',[12] and land trusts. These would be based on the reforms contained in the Green Paper on the Governance of Britain, which would transform the relationship of the executive to Parliament and other areas of government, including the use of petitions to influence policy.[13] At the end of her speech on Confident Communities, Blears noted the ideological basis of this vision for returning power to communities, mentioning the writing of the guild socialist and historian, G. D. H. Cole (1889–1959). She cited a passage from the final sentence of the fifth volume of his magnum opus, *The History of Socialism*, which was published post-humously in 1960. It amounts to a statement of his own ideological position:

> I am neither a Communist nor a Social Democrat, because I regard both as creeds of centralization and bureaucracy, whereas I feel sure that a Socialist society that is true to its equalitarian principles of human brotherhood must rest on the widest possible diffusion of power and responsibility, so as to enlist the active participation of as many as possible of its citizens in the tasks of democratic self-government.[14]

Cole was one of the small group of Guild Socialists who were deeply influenced by political pluralism before the First World War, and who resisted the demands of centralisation and planning.[15] How this relates to the increased nationalisation of policy design and the fixation on audit is an open question. It is highly unlikely that Gordon Brown would regard Cole as an intellectual antecedent.

These initiatives became the substance of *An Action Plan for Community Empowerment: Building on Success*,[16] which was published in October 2007. At her speech to launch the plan,[17] Blears spoke of the 'new localism' involved in participatory budgeting and asset transfer, and in many of the 23 other practical actions proposed in the document. The aim was to make '[d]emocracy everywhere less a monologue, more a conversation, informed and enriched by a diverse range of voices ... And more and more people feeling not sidelined or powerless in the face of change, but with the confidence to say "this is my community, and I'm proud of it".' The *Action Plan* began with the somewhat strange idea of a statutory 'duty to involve'[18] local people in local authority decision making (something which has hitherto been based on the idea of the election of councillors). The rhetoric is dominated by the idea of replacing all 'top down' ways of working with the need to 'access opportunities', including participatory budgeting and charters. Among the 23 policy objectives listed, some were vaguer than others. For instance, there were fairly clear policies on tenant representation in housing management, but extremely nebulous ideas about the need to 'embed community empowerment in cohesion activities', which might involve something called a Citizens' Day.[19] The key policies outlined in the earlier speeches were all fleshed out, but with very few details as to how this would affect local government[20] – the new localism was steered by the centre. The Government's role was that of 'helping to ensure' that there was a response to individual need, with various targets for 'community empowerment for local authorities'. Ultimately this was part of what it called 'the choice agenda and the effective personal tailoring of services', which would at the same time lead to greater community cohesion, increased levels of trust and social capital and a more thriving and participatory local democracy.[21] On the one hand, there is the market-driven ideology of individual services and, on the other, the notion of direct participatory democracy, which may well be at odds with one another. Rights were to be given to various, presumably self-appointed, community activists and entrepreneurs, as well as 'citizens' groups' to coerce local authorities into action.[22] Greater power was also to be given to local government and public involvement in health. What was noticeably lacking was any detailed analysis of the functioning of local democracy and any remedy for the loss of interest in local politics. More well-meaning yet centrally-steered policies creating ever increasing amounts of bureaucratic control of 'local' participation through concordats and agreements do not seem to me the best way of beginning to reinvigorate local politics. An alternative will be to give significant decision-making powers back to municipalities and other local authorities and to move away from seeing the local purely in policy and service-delivery terms – but this would require a degree of trust, a loss of control by the centre, and the possibility of the decision-makers making mistakes.

In her second speech to the LGA in December 2007,[23] Blears spoke of the successes in delivering on the 'new localism', of putting 'some flesh on the bones'. She suggested that there had already been a change in politics as people had become more involved in policy formation and de-livery, which had built on good practice such as 'citizens' panels' and 'planning for real'.[24] She also commented on the new Concordat between local and national govern-ment, which would 'unleash the power of local communi-ties' by balancing rights and responsibilities. Councils would have the right to lead the delivery of public services in their area and shape the future 'without unnecessary direction or control'. Both local and central government would be given the responsibility to 'devolve power and engage and empower communities and individual citizens – in debate and decision making and in shaping and deliver-ing services.' In turn, in delivering this policy the Local Area Agreements would function as the

> key means of agreeing, delivering and monitoring the outcomes for each area which are delivered by local government on its own or in partnership with others. We accept that this objective will require major changes in behaviour and practice from central gov-ernment departments, their agencies, government offices, councils and local partners. We share a commit-ment to leading the effective implementation of the necessary changes.[25]

At the beginning of 2008 Blears claimed that it would be the year for a 'New Deal' for local devolution.[26] To this end, a further document was produced at the beginning of the year, *Unlocking the Talent of our Communities*.[27] This raised questions about encouraging greater participation in the local community and set out the Government's strategy for regeneration, which again was centrally directed through a number of agencies and funds (including the Working Neighbourhoods Fund and the Cities Strategy Pathfinders), rather than through local authorities. Local Area Agreement targets were to be negotiated with the central Government. All this was to

> encourage a greater sense of 'active citizenship' and harness new technology to facilitate greater civic participation and political involvement at the local level. Constitutional renewal and the reform of government institutions will provide increased opportunities and influence for people to be involved in decision-making (nationally and locally), and promote cohesive communities.[28]

This centrally-steered community-building policy was aimed at increasing participation and addressing the perceived problem that only 38 per cent of people felt that they could influence local decisions. Bypassing local government through new partnerships is hardly likely to lead either to increased levels of participation in local government, or to change the demographic profile of those committed to making it function.

Shortly afterwards, in a lecture which amounted to a piece of futurology, 'Five years from now',[29] Blears predicted the likely outcome of this set of policies in terms of the re-invention of the way in which Britain was governed. 'The biggest change,' she felt, would be 'a fundamental and lasting shift in the way local government works with the communities it serves', which would be characterised by a far stronger sense of partnership. There would be increased levels of co-operation between different communities, as well as contracts between councils and communities which would allow communities to organise things for themselves. 'In five years' time', she concluded, 'I hope we can all look back on hard work that will have shaped a stronger, more responsive local democracy, in tune with the needs of our communities, fit for the challenges of the twenty-first century.' Whether the vision will lead to greater participation in the local democratic process and in community activism is an open question. The greatest problem, it seems to me, is the sheer force of Government centralism and the lack of trust in local communities and local government to organise things as they see fit. Unless this crucial issue is addressed, the rhetoric will fall a long way short of the practice.

'The old nationalism'

Despite the new localism, there is little to indicate that the pattern of biennial spending reviews and top-downward policy production and implementation is likely to change significantly, even if there are more people involved in the implementation at the local level. 'Constrained discretion' seems to be so ingrained in the British (or at least the English) system that it is hard to imagine Gordon Brown giving it up in favour of devolution to local communities. As Simon Lee notes: 'His desire to micro-manage and centrally prescribe policy development and resource allocation increasingly placed him within the top-down, technocratic Fabian tradition of Labour modernisers.'[30] NHS reform, which used the rhetoric of local devolution, with Primary Care Trusts based on some degree of local representation and decision-making, has been constantly challenged by Treasury-led national policy directives and standards. This central direction means that local institutions from councils to PCTs to schools simply become deliverers of services with policies and targets (and consequent rewards) set by national Government. 'Clients' are easily redesignated as 'customers' or 'consumers' who want 'choice' in education or healthcare or other service provision (rather than a degree of control or participation over local decisions on priorities).[31] The Government becomes the cox and the agencies (which might range from local councils to 'Third Sector' organisations), the oarsmen.[32] Within such a system there is little space left for local decision-making: deciding whether to use wheelie-bins or black plastic bags or what and how much to recycle hardly amounts to a reinvention of local government. The rhetoric of 'bottom-up' reform and 'flexibility' floundered on the imposition of targets in every imaginable public sector from Health and Safety to education to biofuels. What Simon Lee called the 'essential contradiction' involved in public service reform was that 'constrained discretion could in practice operate only by decreasing the freedom and flexibility of local communities and public spending bodies to make autonomous choices about the design (as opposed to the administration and delivery) of policy.'[33] The tensions are revealed in a speech Brown gave in 2003 to the Social Market Foundation. While speaking of devolution, participation and local autonomy, he nevertheless claimed that 'local autonomy without national standards may lead to increased inequalities between people and regions and the return of postcode lotteries'. The only way of ensuring consistency would be through national targets.[34]

Outside of Scotland, Northern Ireland and Wales, there has been a degree of devolution to Regional Development Agencies which Gordon Brown sees as evidence of unprecedented decentralisation.[35] However, there is little sense of participation in RDAs, and Regional Assemblies ('Councils and Communities in Partnership') have not proved popular, as was evidenced by the fiasco over the proposed referendum for direct election to the North-East Assembly. Although Brown spoke of the reduction in the number of inspections and targets in his speech to the Social Market Foundation, his emphasis remained on devolution of *delivery* rather than formulation of services.

Britain, which had been weakened by the dictum that 'the man in Whitehall knows best', he claimed, would be strengthened by 'local centres awash with initiative, energy and dynamism'. These would be coupled with 'relentless pursuit of stronger markets to maximise efficiency; and in those areas where market failures are chronic, redoubled efforts to pioneer more decentralised systems of public service delivery'.[36]

One of the most bizarre areas of recent policy has been the effort to introduce pseudo-markets and the rhetoric of 'choice' into healthcare and education, as if health and education were commodities to be bought and sold by disinterested consumers. This would imply that schools and hospitals had to be in competition with one another.[37] Brown even went as far as claiming that public services would have to be adapted to meet 'the challenge of ever rising individual aspirations, people's desire for an individual, often personalised tailor-made service'.[38] This combination of policies could lead to an extraordinary set of seemingly conflicting objectives, which Brown outlined (unintentionally) in a speech in March 2007:

> So developing a service that is personal to the citizen's needs, and to the citizen's wishes, will take us in the next few years into exciting and innovative new areas of policy, greater choice, greater competition, greater contestability, there will be greater local accountability, there will be new approaches to the responsibilities as well as to the rights of a citizen, there will be a coming together with the third sector and social enterprise so that we can do far more … So just to summarise, reforms that create greater citizen empowerment and accountability so that people have more control over the services that serve them, greater choice, competition and condensability [sic] so that people have more options from the services that serve them, including from the third sector,

greater workforce empowerment so that public servants can actually gain the satisfaction and the confidence that their talents and their expertise is valued by the whole of the general public, and a focus on responsibilities as well as rights, as we personalise services that are fair to all and personalised to each.[39]

The conflict here, it seems to me, is between the consumption and market choice of goods provided or regulated by the state and participative citizenship – the traditional ethics of service based on voluntary and active participation, which is expanded to include the so-called Third or voluntary sector, is combined with a consumerist and individualist approach. Furthermore, nothing is said about how the different participants in the process, especially those at the local government level, are to make collective decisions.

Being British

The conflict between the 'new localism' and 'constrained discretion' is shown most clearly in the seeming inconsistencies in some of the Government policies on decentralisation. Devolution to Scotland, Wales, London and, most recently, to Northern Ireland, has meant there is significant local control over healthcare, education and many areas of public policy. Even though there are few revenue-raising powers, there is nevertheless a genuine control over resource allocation and policy. According to Anthony King, '[w]ith the coming of devolution to Scotland and Wales, that single locus of sovereign authority no longer exists'.[40] This means that for the most part, policies outside foreign and defence policy are now English rather than British. Given that there is still no English parliament responsible for English policies and Scottish and Welsh MPs have a say over policies which do not affect their constituents, the so-called West Lothian question has become increasingly pressing. It is difficult to justify what might be called the democratic deficit between the different nations of the United Kingdom.[41] It is perhaps because of this inconsistency that politicians, including both Tony Blair and Gordon Brown, have spoken so much about the virtues of Britishness as a way of detracting from the issues.[42]

In many of the statements on Britishness the tensions between the local and the national are highlighted. For instance, in one of his final speeches as Prime Minister, given to the Runnymede Trust on 1 December 2006, entitled 'The Duty to Integrate: Shared British Values',[43] Tony Blair spoke of integration 'at the point of shared, common unifying values'. Following the pattern of many of his earlier speeches, he described these values in terms of 'belief in democracy, rule of law, tolerance' as well as 'respect for this country and its shared heritage'. According to this sort of rhetoric, the *national* rather than the local community functions as the locus for integration. Blair claimed that belonging to this national community requires a minimum set of conditions, including proficiency in English as a common language.[44] At the end of the speech he slips explicitly into the language of national community in terms of the 'duty to integrate':

> If you come here lawfully, we welcome you. If you are permitted to stay here permanently, you become an equal member of our community and become one of us. Then you, and all of us, who want to, can worship God in our own way, take pride in our different cultures after our own fashion, respect our distinctive histories according to our own traditions; but do so within a shared space of shared values in which we take no less pride and show no less respect. The right to be different. The duty to integrate. That is what being British means. And neither racists nor extremists should be allowed to destroy it.

What is important here is the idea of shared space and shared values as a form of unity and diversity. This resembles a speech made by David Blunkett, the former Home Secretary, who claimed at the end of 2001:

> The UK has had a relatively weak sense of what political citizenship should entail. Our values of individual freedom, the protection of liberty and respect for difference, have not been accompanied by a strong, shared understanding of the civic realm. This has to change.[45]

Being British then is about the duty to integrate into a strong civic realm – and that is a duty promoted and sponsored by the national Government. This has been developed at length by Gordon Brown in his many utterances on the subject.

Gordon Brown and Britishness

At the very beginning of the Labour Government in 1997 Gordon Brown, as the new Chancellor of the Exchequer, gave a lengthy lecture for the *Spectator* on Britishness, which he claimed was 'about what Orwell called the British genius'.[46] It would be possible to understand the forces that bound the country together, he held, only by understanding 'our Britishness', that is, those shared values and characteristics of national identity. In this speech, which has provided the blueprint for all his subsequent speeches (sometimes verbatim), he enunciated the key British qualities as 'being creative, adaptable, and outward looking, believing in liberty, duty and fair play', which would provide the resources to face the future. A 'vibrant civil society' would be one in which individualism was properly balanced by the demands of the community and the state:[47] 'a moment's consideration tells us that even Victorian society was grounded in a more complex interplay between the claims of self interest, duty and fairness'.

'Self-help', he went on later in the lecture, 'was not so much a belief in an ethic of self-interest which might benefit only a few but a commitment to an ethic of hard work and self improvement that could unite all.' This meant that 'the British way is not a self-interested individualism but to build a strong cohesive society where there is opportunity for all'. Consequently, he held, 'the essence of Britishness' was to be found in qualities rooted in the history of 'successive waves of invasion, immigration, assimilation and trading partnerships that have created a uniquely rich and diverse culture'.

More recently, in his 2004 speech at the seventieth anniversary of the British Council, Brown similarly noted:

> Out of tidal flows of British history certain forces emerge again and again which make up a characteristically British set of values and qualities which, taken together, mean that there is indeed a strong and vibrant Britishness that underpins Britain.[48]

In 1997 he had summarised these qualities, which 'add up to the British genius' as 'a passion for liberty anchored in a sense of duty and an intrinsic commitment to fair play ... These are the qualities of an old country with the strength to continuously renew itself.'[49] There was a 'golden thread'[50] running through British history 'of the individual standing firm against tyranny and the arbitrary use of power'. This thread, he claimed,

> runs from that long ago day in Runnymede to the bill of rights in 1689 to, not just one, but four great reform acts within less than a hundred years ... The great tradition of British liberty has, first and foremost, been rooted in the protection of the individual against the arbitrary power of the state.

In later speeches a few extra significant events were added, including the abolition of slavery, the Peasants' Revolt and even the Leveller demands during the Civil War for complete equality.[51]

Drawing on something resembling a primitive Whig interpretation of history, Brown has returned to this familiar theme of a golden thread on numerous occasions.[52] At times it is related to liberty, tolerance and religion. Even the Authorised Version of the Bible was an *Eirenicon*:

> It was Montesquieu who wrote in the 18th century that ours was 'the freest country in the world'. I would suggest that it is because different ethnic groups came to live together in one small island that we first made a virtue of tolerance, welcoming and including successive waves of settlers – from Saxons and Normans to Huguenots and Jews and Asians and Afro-Caribbeans, and recognising plural identities. Today 85 per cent believe a strong sense of tolerance is important to our country's success. And I would suggest that out of that toleration came a belief in religious and political freedom – illustrated best by Adam Nicholson's story of the creation of the King James Bible: different denominations coming together in committee to create what was called 'irenicon', which means a symbol of unity for the whole nation.[53]

At the same time, however, the thread was connected with a different set of themes in British history which were focused on common endeavour and shared values. It was thus a

> golden thread which has also twined through it a story of common endeavour in villages, towns and cities, men and women with shared needs and common purposes, united by a strong sense of duty and often an even stronger sense of fair play.

In revolutionary terms, liberty was always balanced by fraternity. In 2006 he made much the same point. There was a

strong sense of duty and responsibility: men and
women who did not allow liberty to descend into a
selfish individualism or into a crude libertarianism;
men and women who, as is the essence of the labour
movement, chose solidarity in preference to selfishness;
thus creating out of the idea of duty and responsibility
the Britain of civic responsibility, civic society and the
public realm.[54]

This led to a balancing of liberty with the ethics of community or 'neighbourliness'. This uniquely British settlement of
'individuals, communities and state' was represented in the

guilds, the charities, the clubs and associations – which
bred amongst other things the City of London's unique
structure – and from the churches, to the municipal
provision of public amenities like libraries and parks
and then to the mutual insurance societies, trades
unions and non governmental organisations, the British
way is to recognise and enhance local initiative and
mutual responsibility in civil affairs and to encourage
and enhance the status of voluntary and community
organisations – Burke's 'little platoons' – in the service
of their neighbourhoods.

The balancing of freedom and responsibility has ensured
that the ideology of excessive state power as well as that of
liberal individualism have never caught on in Britain:

The two ideologies that have dominated the histories
of other countries have never taken root here. On the
one hand an ideology of state power, which choked
individual freedom making the individual slave to some
arbitrarily defined collective interest, has found little or
no favour in Britain. On the other hand an ideology of
crude individualism – which leaves the individual isolated, stranded, on his own, detached from society
around him – has no resonance for a Britain which has

a rich tradition of voluntary organisations, local democracy and civic life.

In his 2004 lecture on Britishness he made similar points, enunciating the British virtues of liberty, duty, fair play and decency, but also recognising the need 'to restore and enhance local initiative and mutual responsibility' by strengthening local government, a subject he had only hinted at in 1997. He went on:

> Rather than asking more people to look upwards to Whitehall to solve all their problems, the British way is surely to encourage more and more people, from their own localities, to take more charge of decisions that affect their lives ... a reinvigorated local democracy can, I believe, emerge to empower people in their own neighbourhoods to deal with the challenges they face.

As in his earlier speech, Brown documented the changes in the concepts of Britishness from the fixed certainties of the late imperialism of the post-War era to the multicultural realities of the present. He lists a number of still relevant attributes based on 'real achievements of the past'. These range from the rejection of arbitrary monarchy, the promotion of liberty and tolerance, the industrial revolution and Empire, the absence of a revolution – a questionable fact in English history – and the lack of a written constitution. Acknowledging the historical research about the creation of a national ideology,[55] he called for 'the recognition of the importance of and the need to celebrate and entrench a Britishness defined by shared values strong enough to overcome discordant claims of separatism and disintegration'. He directed his speech against those who perceived Britain in terms of 'managed decline' and defeatism.[56] His 2004 speech was even more clearly marked by its attacks on the defeatism of so many others who sought to do Britain down.

Throughout his speeches his remedies have remained identical. Coupled with the libertarian and communitarian ethic was the 'commitment to fair play' and 'decency'. This moved beyond 'self-interested individualism' to the idea of the 'helping hand' enunciated by Adam Smith in his *Theory of Moral Sentiments*. This led, he claimed, to what Jonathan Sacks[57]

> captures eloquently for our times when he talks of British society and citizenship not in terms of a contract between people that, in legalistic ways, defines our rights narrowly on the basis of self interest but a British 'covenant' of rights and responsibilities born out of shared values which can inspire us to neighbourliness and service to others.

Later he noted that citizenship would be 'more than a test, more than a ceremony – it is a kind of contract between the citizen and the country, involving rights and responsibilities that will protect and enhance the British way of life'.[58]

In his speeches, Brown defines freedom negatively as freedom from restraint, but also positively in the sense of being free to pursue higher virtues and to gather together for socially desirable goals. This led to an openness and to a creativity and a willingness to experiment. Through this creative common endeavour emerged some of the great British institutions, envied across the world, including the NHS and the Open University. This common purpose was something to be treasured:

> Not the individual on his or her own living in isolation sufficient unto himself but a Britain of creativity and enterprise which is also a Britain of civic duty and public service. And in this vision of society there is a sense of belonging that expands outwards as we grow from family to friends and neighbourhood; a sense of

belonging that then ripples outwards again from work, school, church and community and eventually outwards to far beyond our home town and region to define our nation and country as a society.[59]

This vision was to be expressed through the myriad of small organisations and charities working for the common good: 'The man in Whitehall never knew best; the woman in the WRVS and local community service usually knew much more.' Speaking more practically, Brown mused whether these virtues might be expanded into a new form of community service for young people. A third aspect emphasised by Brown was 'citizenship' and how this was to be defined and symbolised in the new society. He concluded by emphasising that Britain needed to discover again that 'its identity was never rooted just in imperial success or simply the authority of its institutions, nor in race or ethnicity'.

At the beginning of 2006 Brown gave a lecture to the Fabian Society on 'The future of Britishness', where he reflected at length on 'what being British means, what you value about being British and what gives us purpose as a nation', and how this related to the 'modern view of citizenship; the future of local government, ideas of localism; and, of course, our community relations and multiculturalism'.[60] In most ways the lecture is identical to his earlier speeches, but delivered after the 2005 London bombings, it is far more acutely aware of the multicultural nature of British society. Indeed, he said, 'terrorism in our midst means that debates, which sometimes may be seen as dry, about Britishness and our model of integration clearly now have a new urgency'. Further thought, he felt, could have implications for all groups, including the white British community. Instead of retreating into what he called 'exclusive identities rooted in 19th century conceptions of blood, race and territory', he thought the British people should be able to gain great strength from celebrating a British identity which is bigger than the sum of its parts and a union that is strong because of the values we share and because of the way these values are expressed through our history and our institutions.

The question was that of 'how diverse cultures, which inevitably contain differences, can find the essential common purpose without which no society can flourish'.

His remedy was much the same as in his earlier speeches. The British genius consisted in 'creativity, inventiveness, enterprise and our internationalism, our central beliefs are a commitment to liberty for all, responsibility by all and fairness to all'. Being British thus carries responsibilities as well as rights. In a 'modern progressive view of Britishness', Brown claimed,

> liberty does not retreat into self-interested individualism, but leads to ideas of empowerment; responsibility does not retreat into a form of paternalism, but is indeed a commitment to the strongest possible civic society; and fairness is not simply a formal equality before the law, but is in fact a modern belief in an empowering equality of opportunity for all.

This could be achieved, he felt, by breaking up

> in the name of liberty, centralised institutions that are too remote and insensitive and so devolve power; to encourage in the name of responsibility the creation of strong local institutions; and, in new ways in the name of liberty, responsibility and fairness, to seek to engage the British people in decisions that affect their lives.

British values were to be best carried forward by 'local clubs, associations, societies and endeavours – from churches and trades unions to municipal initiatives and friendly societies'. He continued:

While all governments have proved to be cautious in devolving power, I hope we can say that – as the Scottish Parliament, Welsh Assembly and Mayor in London bear witness – this Government has done more to devolve power than any other. But we must now look to further devolution of power away from Westminster, particularly to a reinvigoration of local government and to schools, hospitals and the self management of local services, the emphasis on empowerment, communities and individuals realising their promise and potential by taking more control over their lives.

Brown returned to the theme of what he called a 'British national community service'. This, he felt, would have the function of 'engaging and rewarding a new generation of young people from all backgrounds to serve their communities; demonstrating our practical commitment to a cohesive and strong society'. It was envisaged as a kind of universal gap-year programme not just aimed at middle-class students, which might be sponsored by faith groups and business organisations. Again he raised the theme of citizenship, which would be encouraged in order to ensure a proper balance 'between diversity and integration'. Integration might be encouraged by a British equivalent of Independence Day or Bastille Day, and by giving British history greater prominence in the national curriculum. He concluded:

So, a modern view of Britishness founded on responsibility, liberty and fairness requires us to: demand a new constitutional settlement; take citizenship seriously; rebuild civic society; renew local government; work for integration of minorities into a modern Britain, and be internationalist at all times.

These oft-repeated themes in Gordon Brown's speeches point to a great sense of confusion in Government policy, which relates to the question of how the local is connected to the national. In particular, there is a tension between the demands for devolution and the calls for more local democracy across the country which have led to the establishment of different tiers of participatory democracy in some parts of the United Kingdom, and the idea of a target-driven national community undergirded by shared British values.

Conclusion

It is, of course, easy to criticise Brown for many of his thoughts about shared values. In particular, his conflation of Britishness with Englishness, which is evident from the events he chooses as the hallmarks of the development of British liberty – most obviously the Magna Carta – has been subject to much criticism.[61] But there are far more important questions which relate to a further set of key issues involving the role of the state, particularly in defining and forging values, identities and histories. These are crucial to the success of the promotion of community cohesion and a sense of national identity. The very silly dubbing of low culture as 'Cool Britannia' in the early years of New Labour, epitomised by Union Jacks used as designs on Geri Halliwell's skimpy dress and Noel Gallagher's guitar, would hardly be likely to achieve much by way of serious community cohesion, nor, for that matter, would it boost the vitality of local democracy. It had as much substance as Bruce Forsyth's rendition of 'I'm backing Britain' as a crusading song for Harold Wilson's eponymous campaign of 1968. Football or rugby fans wrapped in St George's flags and drunk on mass-produced second-rate continental beers might be a symbol of something, but it is little more than wishful thinking to suppose it marks any sort of new national identity. And if it does, it strikes me that it is a wholly undesirable form.[62] Flying the flag from public buildings in England on St George's Day is a bizarre move, at least until such time as England has its own devolved parliament.

Something in the rhetoric of national identity is important, and, it seems to me, what is central is the minimum rather than the maximum: instead of talking about British values, what might be more important is to identify the universal practical requirements (British or otherwise) necessary for local participatory democracy to function. In the next chapter I will address how this policy relates to the new localism and in particular the idea of devolution, as well as to the British values spoken of by Brown. In beginning to explore this area I focus on the relationships between the local community and the Government in forging community cohesion. This requires a detailed analysis of the state's role in the policy of creating dialogue between different groups, and it is here that religious identity becomes important.

CHAPTER FOUR

Religion and Community Cohesion

The last two chapters have shown something of the inherent ambiguity in Government policy towards local communities and how these are related to the British state. While there has been much talk of devolution to the local, this has not been accompanied by serious political reform. Indeed, much of the language of national values has tended in the opposite direction. The implications for policy on religion are profound: for many, especially among the non-white communities, religion is one of the key aspects of human and community identity, even if it is not the only way in which local communities identify themselves. Indeed, it is true to say that for the most part religion is principally expressed locally – through the local church or mosque and its associated groups. Religion cannot be relegated to the private sphere but is crucial to public identity. This makes any form of straightforward secularism, where religion is regarded as a private matter of choice, unable to deal effectively with what has usually been dubbed multiculturalism. Where liberal politics has tended to focus public policy on centrally directed policies of anti-discrimination and equality for all members of society,[1] it has been far less interested in group identities expressed locally. Where the individual identifies primarily through a group, which may be first and foremost a religious group (and which embraces a public set of characteristics and identities, and possibly even a system of public law),[2] this creates serious problems for the secular perception of individualised religion. As Tariq Modood writes:

> Marginalized and other religious groups, most notably Muslims, are … making a claim that religious identity, just like gay identity, and just like certain forms of racial identity, should not just be privatized or tolerated, but should be part of the public space.[3]

On purely pragmatic grounds, it seems to me, there is a need to recognise the public nature of religious identity. The boundary lines between public and private in religion are simply not drawn as clearly as liberal multicultural 'neutral space' policy presupposes. This means that members of some minority groups will resort to the decision-making systems of their own (local) communities rather than participate in the neutral (national) public arena. And where this practice becomes controversial and shunned by others – as with much of the anti-sharia law rhetoric of recent years – it can reinforce a separatist and culturally distinctive identity. Cultural and religious identity is thus not politically neutral, but rather a function of the relationships between different groups within society. It is obviously determined by a large number of factors, including religion, but also economic deprivation as well as ethnicity and colour. This has serious implications for the way in which multicultural policy is developed. According to Amartya Sen, there is a need to rethink multiculturalism, both to avoid conceptual disarray about social identity and also to resist the purposeful exploitation of the divisiveness that this conceptual disarray allows and even, to some extent, encourages. What has to be particularly avoided ... is the confusion between multiculturalism with cultural liberty, on the one side, and plural monoculturalism with faith-based separatism on the other. A nation can hardly be seen as a collection of sequestered segments, with citizens being assigned fixed places in predetermined segments. Nor can Britain be seen, explicitly or by implication, as an imagined federation of religious ethnicities.[4]

There are obviously different solutions to this complex set of issues. But, it seems to me, there is a need to rethink the nature of public space and the understanding of religion and cultural identity as a public rather than a private phenomenon. This is a relatively new development since, as I suggested in Chapter 1, before the mass immigration from the 1960s onwards Christianity had effectively been the only public religion, and on the whole it had accommodated itself quite happily to the aspirations of the state. The co-existence of a number of religions raised new questions. As Grace Davie asked in 1994: 'how do we accommodate the religious aspirations of diverse communities within a continent dominated for centuries by one religious tradition rather than another?'[5] Moving beyond Davie, however, I would suggest that these problems raised by minority religions also have implications for those religious people – the remaining members of mainline Christian churches – who have not previously thought of themselves as having marginalized identities. Nowadays, we might suggest, all public religion, including Christianity, even in its established forms, is counter-cultural. That means, as I suggested in Chapter 1, that all religious identity is marginal in contemporary secular society. Mainstream Christians will consequently need to think through the role of their public religious identity in relation to the wider society.

This leads to a number of new questions: how far and in what ways are Christians to allow the wider social and political agendas to determine the decision-making processes of their own churches? To what degree do they have the right to assume that they speak for the majority of the nation when decisions have been taken on a number of moral issues which have not been accepted by the churches? The clash between the secular law and the opposition of the churches can be seen, for instance, in the proposals for continued discrimination against women in the Church of England and other churches, as well as the rights of active homosexuals to enter the ministry – but it manifests itself in different stances on abortion, divorce and other moral issues. This means that there is likely to be conflict and compromise as the wider society ensures that there is a degree of regulation within the cultural and religious groups in order to meet the minimum requirements for freedom, equality and human rights even when this offends the sensibilities of the religious minorities. When it goes against the moral and secular norm, public religious and cultural identity (or what has been called 'groupness') creates a far more complex set of problems than the privatised understanding implied by the liberal idea of universal citizenship. Indeed, citizenship and cultural identity will frequently clash. This means that public marks of cultural distinctiveness – like wearing a headscarf or turban or a British Airways employee wearing a cross – are regarded as political acts, even when they are not necessarily of the 'essence' of a religion.[6] This is less a clash of civilisations and more a conflict over different perceptions of private and public.

Community cohesion

The responses to these issues of the politicisation of religion in multicultural societies have varied in different countries. I have already discussed the French policy of *laïcité* in Chapter 1; this is a highly distinctive approach to cultural diversity. In some other countries, which have traditionally been far more accepting of difference than France, however, there has been a retreat from simple liberal toleration which has allowed minority communities to develop separately. This policy has been criticised for creating ghettoes. This has perhaps been most marked in the Netherlands, traditionally a 'pillarised' society of Protestants and Catholics,[7] where there has been significant criticism of liberal multicultural-ism for failing to halt the rise of an anti-liberal and politi-cised form of Islam which culminated in the murder of the iconoclastic right-wing film-maker Theo van Gogh in 2004. The Dutch response has been to question the earlier policy of state funding for minority schools and broadcast-ing (the so-called *Minderhedennota*).[8] There have even been calls for repatriation of immigrants and asylum seekers. Liberal rational secularism is perhaps not quite so ingrained in Dutch society as its permissive sexual policies might imply.

In Britain too some commentators have suggested that there needs to be a rethink of the policy on multicultural-ism, since it has appeared to foster extremism – as was demonstrated in the London bombings and the foiled plots to destroy aeroplanes – as well as 'no-go areas'. This has not simply come from the usual suspects in the right wing. For instance, in a piece of apocalyptic rhetoric, Trevor Phillips, at the time head of the Commission for Racial Equality, spoke of 'marooned communities' which would 'steadily drift away from the rest of us' into 'crime, no-go areas and chronic conflict'.[9] Similarly, in the plan for the CRE in

2006–7, there was talk about communities drifting 'away from the rest of us, evolving their own lifestyles, playing by their own rules and increasingly regarding the codes of behaviour, loyalty and respect that the rest of us take for granted as outdated behaviour that no longer applies to them.'[10] The problem, Phillips claimed, was not to be solved by a straightforward imposition of liberal values from the centre which might well be counterproductive. Instead, he suggested, '[w]e need to stress how you can bridge between communities – what are the networks, spheres and agents that bring people together?' In his Manchester speech, Phillips consequently spoke of the integration agenda as being crucial after the failure of multiculturalism. He saw the 'three preconditions for an integrated society' as resting in 'equality, participation and interaction'. This amounted to a call for what has been termed 'community cohesion', for enforcing or at the very least encouraging a degree of co-operation and communication or 'bridging' between members of different 'communities'.

The roots of the perceived need for community cohesion extend back at least as far as the beginning of the 1980s and the gradual emergence of the concept of the 'inner city' as a cipher for what John Rex called 'the coexistence of incompatible populations'.[11] Serious problems emerged which resulted in civil unrest in Brixton and Toxteth in 1981. Eventually this led to the establishment of the Inner City Task Forces in 1988 set up by Robert Key and headed by Douglas Hollis, a civil servant and Anglican priest, who was able to draw on the expertise of a number of local groups, including churches and other religious communities, in order to gain an insight into the dynamics of local communities.[12] This was probably the first serious recognition by the government of the role of religion in understanding what was happening at the grass-roots in local communities. It amounts to what Casanova called the 'deprivatisation' of religion as 'the British Government turned to the Church at the end of the 1980s, following the futile and almost catastrophically expensive post-war period of inner-city secular social policy'.[13] While this might be to overstate the case, there was at least an acknowledgement that religion was a complex phenomenon with a public role.

The second key episode in the development of community cohesion policies emerged in January 1989 shortly after the establishment of the Inner City Task Forces, after the book burnings in Bradford following the controversy over Salman Rushdie's *Satanic Verses*. This was followed by the issuing of the *fatwa* by the Iranian religious authorities two years later, which meant that the author was forced into hiding.[14] The problems of the existence of communities holding very different world-views from the secular norm were rapidly brought out into the open. Politicised Islam, which was increasingly associated with the militant regime in Iran, was clearly on the agenda. The Rushdie affair raised significant issues about the limits of tolerance. As Modood writes:

> The ultimate issue that the *Satanic Verses* controversy posed are the rights of non-European religious and cultural minorities in the context of a secular hegemony. It is a time for self-discovery. Is the Enlightenment big enough to tolerate the existence of pre-Enlightenment religious enthusiasm, or can it only exist by suffocating all who fail to be overawed by its intellectual brilliance and vision of Man?[15]

What this controversy clearly implied was that there was a different designation of public and private between secularists and at least some members of religious communities.[16] As Charles Taylor, one of the main philosophical theorists of multiculturalism, writes: 'For mainstream Islam, there is no question of separating politics and religion the way we have come to expect in Western liberal society.'[17]

Some years later there were further examples of what was perceived as the effects of social dismemberment and breakdown in the relationships between communities. This reached a head in violent criminal activities which were classified by the press as 'riots' in Oldham, Burnley and Bradford in 2001, all cities where there were particularly high concentrations of people from Asian backgrounds.[18] The adoption of explicit 'community cohesion' policies in Britain lies in the responses to these events. Indeed, no fewer than five major reports were produced in the early years of the present century which addressed these issues.[19] The term 'community cohesion' itself was used in the reports chaired by John Denham and Ted Cantle. The theory behind the various solutions to what was seen to be the collapse of the bonds between communities in these two reports is based, at least implicitly, on the idea of a decline in social capital at least as this might extend beyond the boundaries of the particular community.

The promotion of community cohesion offers a remedy to social unrest based on greater exchange and interchange ('bridging') between the different cultural, ethnic and religious groups who often live cheek by jowl in British cities. Indeed, rather than understanding the chief causes of unrest to lie in the failures of economic redistribution and inequality of income, which was the traditional understanding of the Marxist left, the conflicts between communities were seen as caused principally by the breakdown in social relations rather than economic factors. Key among theorists of 'community cohesion' was Ted Cantle, chief executive of Nottingham City Council, who was appointed chair of the 'Community Cohesion Review Team' in August 2001. In his later book on community cohesion he makes the distinction between economic and cultural problems clear, differentiating between 'social cohesion', which focuses on economic and structural solutions, and 'community cohesion' which is more explicitly concerned with relations between different ethnic, religious and cultural groups.[20] The central problem for Cantle was the relationships between people from different communities who sometimes led quite segregated lives. As he wrote in the 2001 Report:

> There is evidence to suggest that a considerable amount of volunteering takes place within minority ethnic communities, usually through schools and religious activities. The problem, however, is that these activities tend to be for the benefit of others from the same ethnic group/community.[21]

Although one might ask why this form of self-help activity should necessarily be a problem at all, especially when people might have been excluded by other communities, there is clearly a sense in which communities need to engage in what he called 'inter-cultural collaboration', that is, to communicate across ethnic and religious boundaries if society is to function cohesively.[22]

The Government and community cohesion

After she had been made Secretary of State for Communities, Ruth Kelly developed these ideas on community cohesion into Government policy.[23] This led to the setting up of the 'Commission on Integration and Cohesion' chaired by Darra Singh, in August 2006, which was given a relatively short-term brief to define and report on integration and cohesion. A 'Race, Cohesion and Faiths Directorate' was also set up which was explicitly concerned with policy delivery in the area of equal rights legislation, as well as the promotion of community cohesion, which was defined loosely in terms of a 'shared sense of belonging'. In a list of bullet points, the departmental website goes on to clarify in more detail the characteristics of a cohesive community:[24]

- There is a common vision and a sense of belonging for all communities;
- the diversity of people's different backgrounds and circumstances is appreciated and positively valued;
- those from different backgrounds have similar life opportunities;
- strong and positive relationships are being developed between people from different backgrounds in the workplace, in schools and within neighbourhoods.

The final point implies an increase in social capital (i.e. 'strong and positive relationships') between people from different backgrounds. This ambitious and wide-ranging list of policy objectives forms one part of a broader set of community cohesion policies through all Government departments. Across the board the role of the state is understood as promoting a form of social engineering to ensure that people live in cohesive communities where the different ethnic and religious groups are encouraged, if not forced, to interact with one another. It is considered so important that the idea of community cohesion has been imposed in many areas, including education.[25]

There have been recent efforts to review good practice in community cohesion,[26] as well as the report of the Commission chaired by Darra Singh entitled *Our Shared Future*, published in June 2007.[27] This lengthy document focuses on four areas: shared futures, a new model of rights and responsibilities, a new emphasis on mutual respect and civility, and visible social justice. The definition offered of an 'integrated and cohesive community' in the report is one where:

- There is a clearly defined and widely shared sense of the contribution of different individuals and different communities to a future vision for a neighbourhood, city, region or country;

- there is a strong sense of an individual's rights and responsibilities when living in a particular place – people know what everyone expects of them, and what they can expect in turn;
- those from different backgrounds have similar life opportunities, access to services and treatment;
- there is a strong sense of trust in institutions locally to act fairly in arbitrating between different interests and for their role and justifications to be subject to public scrutiny;
- there is a strong recognition of the contribution of both those who have newly arrived and those who already have deep attachments to a particular place, with a focus on what they have in common;
- there are strong and positive relationships between people from different backgrounds in the workplace, in schools and other institutions within neighbour-hoods.[28]

This list obviously covers concrete redistributive policies and has a strong sense of equal rights in service delivery, as well as a call for 'trust' in local decision-making bodies. At the same time there are vaguer objectives based on the need to interact and promote 'vision' and 'common' identity. Such goals are far more difficult to assess and impossible to quantify, which makes target-setting at the very least problematic.

Complex communities

One of the principal reasons for the difficulties encountered in promoting community cohesion derives from the use of the word 'community' itself. In many documents it is frequently confused and at times little more than a product of the imagination rather than something based on empirical evidence. As far as I have been able to ascertain, nowhere is there a clear definition of what constitutes a community. Sometimes communities are regarded as fixed entities given by ethnic (and often religious) origin rather than groups generated through complex interaction with context.[29] Such uses of the term lack an awareness of the fluctuating and complex nature of ethnic and cultural identity: sometimes, for instance, those who are labelled as belonging to a community having answered a question on an equal opportunities survey may have chosen deliberately to distance themselves from their ethnic or religious 'community'.[30] Although increased levels of participation and interaction between cultural and ethnic communities have become key to the solution to the problem of community cohesion, what is most obvious from the literature is that there is little clarity about what precisely it is that people are supposed to participate in and with whom precisely they are meant to interact.

This problem points to a larger issue. What is left unspoken in most of the discussions and Government literature on community cohesion is any concrete evidence for or even discussion of how people identify themselves. Amartya Sen has noted that there is a tendency to pigeonhole and to categorise people and to define them according to ethnic background or religion. Consequently a country like Britain has a group called 'Muslims' who are understood as principally determined by their religion. And yet it is also clear that there is a huge diversity among Muslims – there are many different types of Muslim, and many may well prefer a different primary identity. Bangladeshis, for instance, will identify themselves quite differently from Pakistanis in relation to their language and the particularity of their culture. Cultural identity is far more complex than simple religious identity: there will often be multiple or hybrid rather than singular identities.

This can work against those who seek simple definitions from different angles. As Sen writes: 'It is, of course, not surprising at all that the champions of Islamic fundamentalism would like to suppress all other identities of Muslims in favour of being only Islamic.'[31] What seems to me to be important is that for much of the time there is not one 'community' through which identity is defined, but a whole range of communities made up of local, national and international ways of identifying oneself. Within each of these identities religion often plays a significant but not always the most important part. As the Parekh report suggested, Britain, like many other countries, is a 'community of communities and individuals'.[32] Such identities might be based, for instance, on language, food, or even musical and aesthetic taste. Identity is not conferred simply by face-to-face contact (along the Putnam model of social capital in *Bowling Alone*) or through a singular ethnic or religious community but can be something far more complex and multi-faceted. As Sen notes, identity may even be something that is chosen.[33]

A visit in May 2007 to Sri Lanka reinforced in me this sense of complex and multi-faceted identities. I was speaking to the clergy of the Anglican diocese of Colombo of the 'Church of Ceylon' (which itself conveys a link with colonial identity).[34] They were Christian priests in a predominantly Buddhist society, but which also has a significant number of Hindus and Muslims. Christians form about 7 per cent of the population, and Anglicans only about 1 per cent. But the identity of the clergy could not be accounted for solely in Christian terms. Ethnically, the clergy comprised Sinhalese, Tamils and a number of Burghers; a few had their first language as English; most spoke Sinhala, although there was a large minority of Tamils, most of whom found Sinhala difficult. The conference had to be conducted in English, a language that had been deliberately suppressed in the earlier period of Sri

Lankan independence from 1956 under the Bandaranaike family. (Solomon Bandaranaike had been raised an Anglican but later vigorously encouraged Buddhism and worked with Buddhist clergy.) Christian identity makes sense only in the context of the history of oppression, particularly of Tamils, which has led to significant levels of civil unrest. Furthermore, even the Christian identity itself was complex: while most clergy were identifiably Anglo-Catholic, some were more Evangelical, depending partly on the legacy of the different Anglican missionary societies, the Society for the Propagation of the Gospel and the Church Missionary Society.

To complicate matters still further, the Church of Ceylon is associated with the former coloniser, and it still controls some of the most elite schools in Sri Lanka. Identities are contested and emerge through interaction and self-definitions, as well as definitions constructed by outsiders. Other shared identities – for instance, love of cricket – displayed something of the way in which cultures or identities are far from static but emerge from dialogue and interaction.[35] Cultural identities combine with histories and myths and narratives, sometimes of liberation from a perceived oppressor, and sometimes in terms of the demonisation of another group. This is obviously true in many other parts of the world. Frequently liberation and demonisation myths combine, as with the Spanish narratives of the expulsion of the Moors, or American or Irish narratives of liberation from the British Crown. Cultural identities are complex and often ambiguous.

The Singh report, *Our Shared Future*, recognises this complexity, emphasising the difficulties involved in analysing modern British identities. 'Increasingly', it claims, 'people are moving away from single identities to multiple identities not just based on race or ethnicity.' This is particularly true of grandchildren of immigrants. According to the report, this is something that can have positive effects,

in that it can prevent any one part of a person's identity becoming prioritised as a source of conflict. Fluid
identities can also act to bring people together as they
discover, for example, experiences common to women
or sporting interests, which cut across other potential
single group conflicts.[36]

What is perhaps most important in this document is the
recognition that the old pattern of clearly demarcated ethnic
and religious identities is breaking down. In the modern
world the effects of globalisation and especially increased
mobility mean that there is a far larger number of countries
represented in the make-up of Britain than only a relatively few years ago. Fluidity and ever-changing identities are
the order of the day.

But what precisely is a community?

Although this issue of complexity has been recognised in
the latest report, what is still far from clear in recent British
multicultural policy is precisely how the term 'community'
is to be understood. 'Community cohesion' implies bridging
between communities as well as building up social capital
within communities.[37] In the modern British context, the
complexity of identity and multiculturalism becomes
especially pressing since, more often than not, the word
'community' when applied to community cohesion is used
to mean something other than faith-based or ethnic communities. According to some of the Government rhetoric,
community is something in which members of *different*
ethnic and faith groups are meant to cohere – it applies
primarily to the new community formed through sharing.
Given that it most frequently points to something which is
wider than the various local ethnic communities, 'community' is used in a very different way from the sort of

face-to-face community founded on blood and soil envisaged by Tönnies (discussed in Chapter 2). As *Our Shared
Future* puts it:

> The social capital in a community is linked to the
> strength of its social networks between people. There
> are two types of social capital: bonding social capital is
> about networks of similar people such as family mem-
> bers and friends from similar backgrounds; and bridging
> social capital refers to relations between people from
> different backgrounds. Both forms of social capital
> benefit a community and its members, but only bridg-
> ing capital is about people from different groups getting
> on (key to our measure of cohesion) – although we
> have found that bonding capital can give people the
> confidence they need in order to bridge.[38]

The idea of *bridging* social capital makes these new sorts of
communities much more like Tönnies' version of society.[39]

In a report which is about *community* cohesion, it is
nevertheless surprising that there is so little consistency
between the 318 uses of the word 'community'. These vary
from local and religious groups to something much wider.
The confusion is clear from one particular paragraph: while
stressing that the policy of community cohesion should be
'driven by a whole community approach', at the same time
it claims that 'relationships with Muslim communities may
have accelerated this debate, but we would ask for a whole
community approach to be the driving force of central
Government engagement on integration and cohesion'.[40]
How precisely these two types of community are to be
related is not clearly outlined.

Another recent example reveals a similar vagueness in
the use of the word: despite 134 occurrences of the word
'community' throughout the document, the Government's
lengthy Sustainable Communities five-year plan nowhere
offers a definition of a community, apart from identifying it

with a particular geographical place. The closest it comes to any clarity is where it differentiates communities from neighbourhoods ('the areas which people identify with most'), which may not be particularly helpful.[41] Similarly, in the White Paper, *Strong and Prosperous Communities*, published in October 2006,[42] there is an interesting section on naming the new 'Parish Councils' which are to deliver services at the most local level. These will be called either parish, town or city councils, but also community, village or neighbourhood councils.

Another highly instructive example of confusion about what is meant by 'community' is displayed by the 'Belonging to Blackburn with Darwen' Local Strategic Partnership[43] campaign, which features as one of the flagship examples of community cohesion planning in the Local Government Association's *Community Cohesion Action Guide* produced in 2004.[44] The Blackburn with Darwen LSP has focused on the 'many lives … many faces … all belonging to Blackburn with Darwen'. It featured 'local people saying why they are proud to belong to the borough'. All these citizens had signed up to what was called a 'charter of belonging'. It was noted in the document that '[t]his formal charter was signed by the members of the LSP, and a shorter summary was distributed across the borough so that the spirit of the charter is available to all'.[45] In this example, the community is something to which one subscribes through some sort of explicit declaration of shared values. It would also appear to be coterminous with a geographical and government entity of relatively recent origin, namely the Borough of Blackburn with Darwen.

On this sort of model of community cohesion, however, little is said about those who choose not to avail themselves of this spirit of belonging, or who do not wish to sign the charter. It is hard to know what room is made for those who simply do not wish to become members of a cohesive community identified with a local government area. (It would incidentally be equally hard for me to understand how I might 'belong' to South Oxfordshire, another recent entity, whose offices are in what is, at least historically, Berkshire, and which provides certain services.) The rhetoric of community is underpinned by constitutional (and occasionally historical) myths of belonging to a particular place, as with many examples in the Local Government Association's *Action Guide*. Yet there is little serious thought about how belonging might be encouraged through political participation in decision-making rather than a vague sense of 'belonging'. Yet within the very same *Guide* there is also much use of the word 'community' in relation to the different ethnic and religious groups that make up the larger 'community'. At other times the official documents discuss the physical surroundings which make the very existence of community possible – in the Five-year Plan, for instance, there is a moving story about Constantine Blake, the first park ranger in St Agnes Park, Bristol, who talks about 'creating space for a community': 'I made [the park] a space the community could use – it's their decision on how they want to use it.' Clearing away drug litter made space for the possibility of social interaction and community cohesion, but it is unlikely that litter-clearing will more generally create many vacuums to be filled by communities.[46]

Conclusion

What has emerged in recent Government policy, as well as in the recommendations coming out of *Our Shared Future*, is that there need to be ways in which *many* communities can become *one* community, albeit one characterised by diversity.[47] All people, regardless of their background, ethnicity or religion, are to have equal access to the political system as well as to the educational and social services of the state. To this end, all local authorities are required to have a community cohesion policy, and are encouraged to measure and quantify their practices in accord with explicit criteria. There is already a substantial body of literature in this area and there are some clearly measurable statistics. But what is completely lacking is a clear definition of what a cohesive community might look like, which means that there can be no adequate criteria for success. *Our Shared Future* speaks frequently in terms of measuring the success of community cohesion (especially in §4), but this rather begs the question about what precisely is being measured and how it relates to other variables such as economic and social deprivation and poverty. Indeed, as some commentators from the Old Left have noted, the community agenda, based on the social capital model, may serve to mask some of the other social inequalities and conflicts in the quest for what might be regarded as perhaps premature harmony. There is much that is laudable and impressive in the community cohesion policy, but the rhetoric and ethics of community can perhaps sometimes be a distraction from the more material causes of deprivation and inequality.[48]

More crucially, however, what still needs to be discussed in detail is the way in which community cohesion requires a reorientation of the structures of politics: *Our Shared Future* speaks of the need to reinvigorate local politics, but it is short on concrete proposals about how this might be done. It scarcely addresses the question of whether the goal of community cohesion in 'promoting meaningful interaction' between groups might best be achieved through reforming the processes of participatory democracy rather than trying to create senses of belonging to Britain or Blackburn or anywhere else. Indeed, the Singh report is resigned to the centralised regime of the Government, acknowledging that 'performance regimes have become a key tool of central government in driving local change. Strong cohesion targets would be an obvious mechanism for all local areas to respond to their local challenges.' It thus recommends that 'there should be a single national PSA target for community cohesion, measured consistently over a reasonable length of time in order to determine national trends'. At the same time it suggests (rather more radically) that

> Local areas should be encouraged to develop their own local indicators of integration and cohesion. These would not be monitored nationally, but could be included in local strategies and plans.[49]

This idea of not monitoring would require a reform of the way in which politics is done – and that would mean a redirection of power and trust to the local area. To take this much further would be nothing short of a form of pluralism, which is what will be outlined in the next chapter in dialogue with Rowan Williams. Integration and cohesion might best be achieved by encouraging and allowing local communities to decide matters for themselves without imposing an agenda from the centre; and where that brings conflict with other communities – as surely it frequently must – this will not be solved through a citizens' day or community day (although they might help), but by forcing a sometimes painful compromise through a meaningful political process with clout. Rather than the 'duty to integrate', as Tony Blair put it,[50] the multicultural policy of community cohesion might be best delivered by redirecting energy to the creation of structures which encourage participation – and that can only be done by giving them power. This leads on to the idea of an 'interactive pluralism', which will be discussed in the next chapter.

CHAPTER FIVE

Rowan Williams and the Politics of Interactive Pluralism

On 7 February 2008 Rowan Williams, Archbishop of Canterbury and the most senior religious figure in England, gave a lecture at a series hosted by the Royal Courts of Justice entitled 'Civil and Religious Law in England: a Religious Perspective'.[1] It provoked a storm of protest from many different quarters, principally because he had appeared to defend parallel legal systems and the use of sharia law to resolve certain disputes in Muslim communities.[2] Trevor Phillips, chairman of the Equality and Human Rights Commission, claimed that the 'The Archbishop's thinking here is muddled and unhelpful'. Raising the idea of separate treatment would 'give fuel to anti-Muslim extremism and dismay everyone who is working towards a more integrated society.' He concluded, 'I don't doubt the Archbishop's desire to accommodate diversity, but we cannot do so at the expense of our common values.' Khalid

Mahmood, Labour MP for Birmingham Perry Barr, thought it

> very misguided. There is no half-way house with this. What part of Sharia law does he want? The sort that is practised in Saudi Arabia, which they are struggling to get away from? Muslims do not need special treatment or to be specially singled out. This would not contribute to community cohesion.

Others, including Gordon Brown, Tony McNulty, Home Office Minister, and Nick Clegg, the recently elected leader of the Liberal Democrats, were equally critical of the apparent denial of one law for all. One of the few defenders of the Archbishop was Mohammed Shafiq, press spokesman of the Ramadhan Foundation for Muslim youth, who thought that the

> comments further underline the attempts by both our great faiths to build respect and tolerance. Sharia law for civil matters is something which has been introduced in some western countries with much success; I believe that Muslims would take huge comfort from the Government allowing civil matters being resolved according to their faith.[3]

Rowan Williams' predecessor, George Carey, entered the debate with two newspaper articles, one in the *News of the World* and the other in the *Sunday Telegraph*,[4] which accused Williams of promoting ghettoisation. Possibly the most unpleasant response was from Andrew Brown in the *Guardian* who accused Williams of living in an academic ghetto that made him too arrogant to acknowledge how the lecture might be received:

> Ignoring the fact that there are some things an archbishop just can't say is all of a piece with the arch-bishop's previous record of silly-clever arrogance

[85]

under fire. I don't mean that he is afraid of martyrdom. On the contrary; he is almost too fond of it and once he has arranged himself in the position of the long-suffering good man, helpless in the hands of his enemies, he seems to forget that he has led the people who trusted him into the same mess, and they didn't ask to be martyred.[5]

Much of the other reaction expressed something of the fear of Islam and the loss of Christian values. This was especially true of voices from the political right. Mark Pritchard, Conservative MP for the Wrekin and a great advocate of Britain as a Christian land,[6] thought that the lecture was 'naive and shocking' and that the Archbishop 'should be standing up for our Judeo-Christian principles that under-pin British criminal law that have been hard fought for'. And yet, when carefully analysed, Williams' Royal Courts Lecture was an intelligent and wide-ranging discussion of some of the key issues involved in the reciprocal relation-ships between religious communities and the wider society. It is part of a long-term project of what he has called 'Interactive Pluralism', which has characterised his thinking for well over 20 years. It seems to me that the Archbishop's thoughts on multiculturalism provide a way forward for addressing – and perhaps even resolving – the key issues which have been raised through the course of this book. The legitimacy of the claims of the nation state over its citizens is central to his long-standing political theory, which has more recently been related to the rights of reli-gious and cultural communities for self-determination and decision-making powers. This chapter discusses the evolu-tion of Williams' political thought before moving on to a discussion in the next chapter of how the sort of pluralism he develops applies to religious communities.

The background to Williams' political thought

In 1984, Rowan Williams wrote an essay on 'Liberation Theology and the Anglican Tradition' where he discussed the impact of what was then a relatively new theological movement and how it might affect the Church of England. In what was a wide-ranging and ambitious essay, he delineated a number of obvious differences between English Anglicanism and the sort of political theology that had developed in Latin America. First, he noted the established nature of the Church of England and the 'assumption of *absolute givenness* in the political structure'.[7] On this sort of model, which was obviously central to the origin of the Church of England in its break with Rome, and which was maintained in the nineteenth century by F. D. Maurice (among many others), the church cannot govern 'precisely because it is *not* a body separable from the state'.[8] For much of Anglican history, there was a harmonious and singular vision of church and state as one body, which Paul Avis referred to as the 'Erastian' paradigm.[9] Critics of this tradition gradually emerged in the late nineteenth century and early twentieth centuries, many of whom, including Charles Gore and other Anglo-Catholics, clamoured for what they called a 'free church in a free state'.[10] This separatist movement obviously carried with it certain political implications.

According to Williams, the most important theorist in this development was the scholar-monk, John Neville Figgis, who differentiated between two forms of political authority.[11] On the one hand, he described a form of absolutist sovereignty which manifested itself in the idea that all forms of association – including the church – were granted by the sovereign's will.[12] On the other hand, however, he also outlined a theory of association where the voluntary corporation rather than the sovereign state was understood as the primary political unit. On this model, Williams writes:

> State authority simply means that, in an association of such associations (an association essentially fluid and dependent upon a variety of factors such as language or geography), power is delegated to the unifying structure in order to balance the claims and order the relations of the smaller units. In this perspective rights can, in certain circumstances, be claimed against the state, because the sovereign state power is not their source.[13]

For Figgis, as for Williams, federalism and decentralisation become the hallmarks of such a system of politics, political arrangements which were hinted at in the conciliar movements of the fourteenth and fifteenth centuries.[14] Although the Reformation period saw a resurgence and to some extent a triumph of absolute sovereignty, particularly among rulers like Henry VIII, Francis I and Philip II, Williams suggests (again with Figgis) that the religiously monolithic state had completely broken down since the Enlightenment. This means that in the modern world churches – including state churches like the Church of England – have become voluntary organisations to which nobody can be compelled to belong. Consequently, Williams claims, the only 'ground upon which the Church of England can now justify its existence … is a federalist theory of ecclesiastical unity and authority'. This carries with it implicit political implications, since, as Williams puts it, '[w]e cannot consistently be federalists in our ecclesiology and absolutists in our politics'. For this reason, he suggests provocatively: 'It might even be said that the Anglican Christian has a peculiarly direct reason for adopting a strongly syndicalist view of political power and of the rights of associations over against an encroaching state.'[15] And it need hardly be said that for an Archbishop in an established church, this is a very bold claim indeed (although admittedly he said it a long time before he was elevated to Canterbury). Even in 1984, then, there were tendencies in Williams' thought towards the elevation of the rights of the association against the universalism of the state.

In such a system, the state's role is to work out a system of justice and to 'rectify imbalances' between the groups. The state thereby becomes an arbitrator rather than a sovereign, since power and decision-making are decentralised. This means, according to Williams, that Figgis turns the Anglican synthesis of church and state on its head. Gone are the old organic unity and pre-established harmonies of sovereign state and established church, and in their place emerges a political system which is more about negotiation and pluralism than absolutism and sovereignty. What this reveals is that Williams' 1984 essay provides a preliminary statement of a number of guiding themes that have shaped his approach to theology and political theory ever since,[16] and which have re-emerged in his time as Archbishop. However – and this is hardly surprising – in 1984 there is no mention of Islam or other religions.[17] In the intervening quarter century or so there has been a recognition by many church leaders of the importance of the need to understand and engage with the other faith communities present in the multicultural society of contemporary Britain. It would be fair to say that in his application of pluralist thought to modern society, Williams has been one of the first Christian leaders to move to a level of sophisticated theological and political thought about multiculturalism. Indeed, his thought is perhaps significantly more sophisticated than what is found in most – and possibly all – of the Government documents.

Nevertheless, despite the changes of the past 20 years, there is a strong sense of continuity in Williams' writings. He remains deeply inspired by Figgis and other pluralists and has acknowledged this explicitly in some of his recent lectures on multi-faith society in modern Europe. Although he no longer uses the term 'syndicalism' – which is probably just as well, given its association with anarchism – there is much in his theory of what he calls 'interactive pluralism' that owes its origin to the English pluralist tradition of the early twentieth century. For instance, in a lecture given to the European Institutions in 2005, Williams writes:

> If the state has no sacred character, it is not the sole source of legitimate common life: intermediate institutions, guilds, unions, churches, ethnic groups, all sorts of civil associations, have a natural liberty to exist and organise themselves, and the state's role is to harmonise and to some degree regulate this social variety. This 'interactive pluralism', rooted in the liberalism of thinkers like Acton, Maitland and Figgis, would see the healthy state neither as a group of suspiciously co-existing groups, nor as a neutral legal unit whose citizens all possessed abstractly equal rights, but as a space in which distinctive styles and convictions could challenge each other and affect each other, but on the basis that they first had the freedom to be themselves.[18]

This consistent programme of interactive pluralism provides a method for critiquing the theories of sovereignty which have survived intact in Government policy in recent years, but also offers a way forward for communities in relation to the state.

Interactive pluralism

The clearest exposition of 'interactive pluralism' that Williams has offered so far during his time as Archbishop is his David Nicholls Memorial Lecture, 'Law, Power and Peace: Christian Perspectives on Sovereignty', which was given in September 2005.[19] Williams used Nicholls' own discussions of Figgis and other pluralists including Nicholls himself[20] to outline his own approach to the relationship between the state and what he calls 'first-level' associations,[21] which amount to something like the small-scale face-to-face communities outlined above in Chapter 2. Regarding Figgis and others as still offering a 'powerful analysis',[22] he observes that the role of the state is principally that of brokerage between 'first-level' associations when there are difficulties and disputes. In this way it provides

> the stable climate for all first-level communities to flourish and the means for settling – and enforcing – 'boundary disputes' between them. The law does not attempt total regulation of how these communities govern themselves (though it may, as with British charity law, require certain standards of accountable practice).[23]

This means that the lawful democratic state is not concerned principally with a delegation of authority from above, but rather with ensuring that the interests of the 'first-level' communities are 'both recognised and effectively brokered, so that none of these communities is threatened in its pursuit of the social good by others'.[24] Because it is no longer an absolute, this means, according to this pluralist model, that

> the lawful state embodies the possibility of its being held to account; it denies its own invulnerability from criticism. Its sovereignty is not a claim to be the source of law, but the agreed monopoly of legal force and a recognition of where the ultimate court of appeal is to be located for virtually all practical and routine purposes.[25]

The state thus exists in virtue of the free consent of the members of the 'first-level' organisations who have accorded to it the role of arbitration and balance. It will facilitate 'co-operation through its own sponsorship and partnership'.[26] In turn this leads on to a kind of subsidiarity but – and here it stands in contrast to the use of the word in most British political discourse – a form of subsidiarity in which the direction of delegated power is always upwards rather than downwards.[27]

The role of the state in a complex society will thus be twofold: first, it will have an interest 'in securing the liberty of groups to pursue their own social goods', and secondly, it will have 'an interest in building in to its own processes a set of cautions and defences against absolutism'.[28] The lawful state ensures that basic human dignity is preserved and life is safeguarded. It guards against what has been called 'repressive tolerance', that is, as Williams suggested (in a different context) 'an intellectually idle and morally frivolous prohibition against raising uncomfortable questions' about truth. Never, however, can the state be regarded as the sole source of authority or truth or beyond criticism. This means that its 'sovereignty is not a claim to be the source of law, but the agreed monopoly of legal force and a recognition of where the ultimate court of appeal is to be located for virtually all practical and routine purposes'.[29]

Within this pluralist system the role of the church and the Christianity it represents is complex. Williams regards the political role of churches as principally that of deflating the claims of the state, of reminding it that its role is primarily that of negotiation or balance rather than sovereignty or command. He claims that no state can ever be accorded absolute authority for one simple reason:

> The Christian tradition rests upon a strong conviction that no political order other than the Body of Christ can claim the authority of God; and the Body of Christ is not a political order on the same level as others, competing for control, but a community that

signifies, that points to a possible healed human world. Thus its effect on the political communities of its environment is bound to be, sooner or later, sceptical and demystifying.[31]

The true sovereign is Christ and no other claims to authority can ever hope to compete. Indeed, Williams regards this as inherent in Christianity through history, even when it has appeared most authoritarian. As he claimed in a recent lecture given in Liverpool on 'Europe, Faith and Culture':

Christianity might have been the system taken absolutely for granted by the society of Western mediaeval Europe, but it still contained the seeds of deep cultural unease, an irony and a scepticism about existing situations and systems in the light of God's action in the cross of Jesus and the revelation of what God's justice really meant.[32]

In the end, it was the cross that led to the sceptical tendency in all Christianity. This meant that the Christian should be 'wary of any such universal sovereignty as of any sacred claims for this or that national polity. There is, ultimately, only one sovereignty which is theologically grounded, and that is Christ's.'[33] Consequently, according to Williams, there would always be an ambiguity in the relationship between church and state. It comes as no surprise that he writes: 'Christianity has a mixed history of relation with political power. It has always been a complex balance.'[34] It needs both to engage with power, but also to retain a sceptical distance. In this way it becomes a kind of critical friend or conversation partner with the state and its laws.

Williams' political theology follows in the same direction as much of his other writing. He frequently talks about the need to question power and certainty wherever they might be found, including in the church and theology. In a 1989 lecture, for instance, he claimed that the shape of the Christian faith is the anchoring of our confidence beyond what we do or possess, in the reality of a God who freely gives to those needy enough to ask; a life lived 'away' from a centre in our own innate resourcefulness or meaningfulness, and so a life equipped for question and provisionality in respect of all our moral or spiritual achievement: a life of *repentance in hope*.[35]

This vision is one of humility, a letting go before the God who simply cannot be controlled, but who constantly draws us onwards in hope. Similar themes emerged in his very first public letter as Archbishop of Canterbury for Christmas 2002:

Faced with the fullness of God in the embryo, the baby, the tired wanderer in Galilee, the body on the cross, we have to look at ourselves hard, and ask what it is that makes us too massive and clumsy to go into the 'little space' where we meet God in Jesus Christ.

According to Williams, it is simplicity and humility that will stifle arrogance as we approach the cross. Criticism of theological and political absolutism in all their guises is thus an implication of the Christian faith. In a programmatic essay written for the 150th anniversary of the beginning of the Oxford Movement, he was critical of the political dimension of the clamour for finality, seeking to open all secular and religious ideologies to 'persistent critical negation' in order to rid the world of the products of what he called the 'destructive longing for final clarity, totality of vision, which brings forth the monsters of religious and political idolatry'.[36]

Given his denial of absolutism and sovereignty, it is hardly surprising that Williams has an ambiguous relationship with political liberalism. In particular, he is deeply suspicious of universalistic versions of liberalism which suppose that the liberal state has the responsibility to dictate and define all forms of human identity in terms of a monolithic centrally-imposed system. In his Chatham Lecture given at Trinity College, Oxford, for instance, he characterises the problems of secularism:

> What we see, in the actual policies of some states and in the rhetoric of the political classes in other states, is a presumption that the rational secular state is menaced by the public or communal expression of religious loyalty ... Conviction is free – that is a foundational principle of modern liberal society; but visible and corporate loyalty to the marks of such conviction ... puts in question the neutrality of the public space and can be read as a sort of aggression against other convictions or against the programmatic absence of convictions that the state assumes for public purposes. For statutory authority to collude with, let alone actively support these loyalties fatally compromises the very basis of legitimate liberal society.[37]

At the same time, however, Williams recognises that the critical impulse behind 'interactive pluralism' also emerges from the questioning of authority which has been the great triumph of the political liberalism which emerged in Europe in the Enlightenment, but which has its seeds much earlier in history. Indeed, he claims, what is best in liberalism is what is best in Christianity, since ultimately interactive pluralism is founded on Europe's Christian heritage. He consequently writes of the virtues of political liberalism, that they

> will survive best if they are seen as the outgrowth of the historic European tensions about sovereignty, absolutism and the integrity of local communities that were focused sharply by the Christian Church and its theology – a theology that encouraged scepticism

about any final political settlement within history.[38]

An ironic detachment from all systems is thus at the heart of Christian political theology. This results in the 'readiness to question in the name of a something more that God alone opens up and makes possible'. Williams consequently suggests:

> Christian faith tells us that, because God is to be trusted, we can be very bold indeed about the degree of scepticism we give to what is less than God. In the context of faith, this is the 'unbearable lightness' that is given us in relation to the systems and expectations of the world around, the irony that is still compatible with love and commitment in God's name.[39]

At the same time, the Christian faith in the equality and dignity of all human beings as created in the image of God helps guard against the loss of a conviction that there is a 'common hope and vocation for human beings, such that the welfare or salvation of one section of humanity cannot be imagined as wholly different from or irrelevant to that of the rest of the race'.[40]

According to Williams' understanding of theology, the political role of the church is understood principally as that of calling the state to account by 'obstinately asking the state about its accountability and the justification of its priorities'. The liberal state is thus obliged to listen if it is not to turn secularism into 'another tyranny'.[41] Here again Williams moves to a discussion of the role of the state as mediator and 'space-maker' rather than sovereign. The key role of the church is to ensure that the state claims nothing more. If that is the case then the state will be primarily that place

> in which mediation and mutual listening will be normal ... If religious communities are acknowledged as participants in public argument, they are bound to

> some level of creative engagement with each other
> and with the secular voice of the administration, so as
> to find a solution that has some claim to be just to a
> range of communal interests.[42]

The alternative, which is maintained by those who regard
religious communities as little more than private arrangements between consenting adults, will lead to exclusion
and ghettoisation, even to what Michael Nazir-Ali, the
Bishop of Rochester has recently called 'no-go areas' in
words reminiscent of Trevor Phillips. Nazir-Ali's solution
amounts to a return to Christianity as the historic English
public faith with little regard to pluralism or seeing other
religions as 'first-level' communities of equivalent status.[43]
This was a criticism that Williams himself recognised:
'Pluralism as a strategy ... can look like a betrayal of what
most Christians would still see as a central affair in their
commitment.'[44]

In distinction, Williams holds that what is key to
human identity is not a vague sense of Britishness or
Europeanism, but a solidarity that emerges from the 'first-
level' association which is the primary unit of socialisation.
For many, this is very likely to be their religion. Thus he
writes:

> The faith community – like other self-regulating com-
> munities – has to be seen as a partner in the negotia-
> tions of public life; otherwise, the most important
> motivations for moral action in the public sphere
> will be obliged to conceal themselves; and religious
> identity, pursued and cultivated behind locked doors,
> can be distorted by its lack of access to the air and the
> criticism of public debate.[45]

Interactive pluralism thus becomes a way to ensure participation in the political process by respecting other cultures
and religions as agents of identity, and drawing them into a

wider debate negotiated cautiously by the institutions of the state, most obviously the democratic process itself, at the local, national and international levels. As Williams put it in his Chatham lecture:

> Loyalty to a sovereign authority is replaced by or recast as identification with a public process or set of public processes; the simple question about loyalty, 'Are you with us or against us?' becomes a question about adequate and confident participation in a law-governed social complex.[46]

In this way, European politics will mature into what Williams calls 'effective partnership with the component communities of the state, including religious bodies'. European politics, he claims, will thus

> try to avoid creating ghettoes. It will value and acknowledge all those sources of healthy corporate identity and political formation (in the widest sense) that are around ... By holding the space for public moral argument to be possible and legitimate, it reduces the risk of open social conflict, because it is not content to relegate the moral and the spiritual to a private sphere where they may be distorted into fanaticism and exclusion. For Europe to celebrate its Christian heritage in this sense is precisely for it to affirm a legacy and a possibility of truly constructive pluralism ... And for the Church to offer this to Europe (and from Europe to the wider world) is not for it to replace its theology with a vague set of nostrums about democracy and tolerance but for it to affirm its faithfulness to the tradition of Christian freedom in the face of the world's sovereignties.[47]

As will be shown in the next chapter, it is in this broader context of 'interactive pluralism', particularly as it relates to Islam, that Williams' Royal Courts Lecture needs to be understood. At the same time it is interesting to note that he has begun to adopt a similar approach, using what he calls 'broadly constructive pluralism', in his efforts to reconcile the different factions in the Anglican Communion. Here too he is seeking to balance the demands of the particular provincial and national churches with the needs of the worldwide Communion by creating space for discussion and debate. Commenting on the conflicts in the Communion in his address to the General Synod of the Church of England in November 2005, he explained 'interactive pluralism' as 'a situation in which difference is publicly acknowledged and given space, but not regarded as an excuse for "ghettoisation" or exclusion from a serious degree of shared work, shared resources and mutual responsibility'.[48] Interactive pluralism is consequently hard work and requires constant testing. It will usually be accompanied by a great deal of conflict. And yet it offers a way forward for multicultural policy (and for much else besides).

CHAPTER SIX

Islam, the Archbishop and the Future

Rowan Williams' Royal Courts Lecture, 'Civil and Religious Law in England: a Religious Perspective'[1] followed the pattern of many of his earlier lectures which were discussed in the last chapter. In particular, it touched on the themes of sovereignty, especially as expressed through law. Williams' primary aim was to ensure that dialogue with Islam is maintained as the pluralist state negotiates space for all religious groups to participate in the political process without losing their public identity. This process is a highly complex problem: negotiating space for the self-expression of religious communities to organise themselves according to their own sets of principles needs to be balanced by the need to protect individual freedom and human rights. This problem, however, does not apply simply to the so-called 'minority religions'. Although he was specifically addressing Islam, Williams' lecture has implications for any faith group, including the Christian churches. My sense is that Rowan Williams long ago faced up to the reality that Christianity was a minority religion. This recognition may have come from his prophetic Scottish Episcopalian teacher, Donald Mackinnon. Mackinnon spoke of the loss of the sort of invulnerability that came with establishment and the probability of 'flirting with obscurity'.[2]

As I showed in Chapter 1, in contemporary Britain all faith groups are 'first-level associations'. This means that all churches are voluntary organisations, even if some have historic privileges and legal protection. Given the low level of churchgoing and its continued decline, what needs to be stressed is that in modern Europe all religious communities are minority communities. This means that they are forced to co-exist and engage with one another and with the wider secular realm, but always within certain parameters which are circumscribed and negotiated with the state. At the same time, however, 'first-level' associations are public and political rather than private societies. They provide a primary – sometimes the only – source of socialisation and identity which makes them inherently public and political. This means that the secular solutions which privatise religion, and which have been adopted, for instance, in France, will inevitably be inadequate.

Despite the nostalgic attachment to establishment by many, especially in certain parts of the Church of England, and the implausible designation of a 'Christian Europe' by others (including Pope Benedict),[3] Williams holds that in practice all religions will need to recognise their minority status.[4] This makes criticism from within the Church at the very least disingenuous, since all religious people are in practice in much the same boat. In his ill-judged article following the Royal Courts Lecture in the *Sunday Telegraph*,[5] for instance, George Carey concluded with an aside that, since Muslims constitute a mere 3 per cent of the population, the proposals set out by Williams would be like using a 'sledgehammer to crack a nut'. What he fails to observe, however, is that this percentage is higher than the number of practising Anglicans.

Williams' question is thus vital for all religions. He consequently asks 'what degree of accommodation the law of the land can and should give to minority communities with their own strongly entrenched legal and moral codes'. On the model of interactive pluralism outlined in the last chapter, this problem affects Christians as well as members of the other faiths, since Christians too are inevitably a 'minority community'.[6] As Williams wrote earlier in his Chatham lecture:

> the Church as a political agent has to be a community capable of telling its own story and its own stories, visible as a social body and thus making claims upon human loyalty. While not a simple rival to the secular state, it will inevitably raise questions about how the secular state thinks of loyalty and indeed of social unity or cohesion. To this degree, it is not in a different case from the Muslim Umma.[7]

In the complex society of modern Britain the answers to the problems of multiculturalism cannot be straightforward. In particular, any discussion of Islam is especially sensitive, as is demonstrated by the near hysteria that greeted the Royal Courts Lecture. However, the lecture fits into Williams' overall political framework. While complex, his central argument is clear. First, drawing on recent scholarship, he shows that sharia law is not a monolithic system but is always related to its broader context. It has always had to be adapted to cultural conditions which means that there does not have to be a 'standoff between two rival legal systems when we discuss Islamic and British law'. Secondly, Williams notes, wherever there is a recognition that Islam co-exists alongside other faiths (and none), then any acceptance of sharia law will need to take account of this minority status. Accepting sharia law will need to be a free choice on the part of those belonging to the Islamic community (and the same would hold true for members of other religions in choosing to accept their own laws). Drawing on the writings of Tariq Ramadan, one of the leading theorists of Islam in the West, Williams had earlier made this point in his lecture on 'Religion, Culture, Diversity and Tolerance':

> There is, says Ramadan, no single 'homeland' for Muslims: they can be at home in any geographical and political environment, and they need to avoid 'self-ghettoisation', becoming 'spectators in a society where they were once marginalized'. They need to be arguing and negotiating in the public sphere.

Ramadan even suggests that Islam shares a similar critique of the state to Christianity. He writes: 'the Muslim distinction between religious and social authority, between what is enjoined for the good of the soul and what is ordered for the stability of an external environment, is really much the same as the Christian distinction between Church and state.' Islam is not restricted to primitive and fundamentalist forms. Instead, Williams claims:

> commitment to the lawfulness of the processes of argument in a society and acceptance of the outcome of ordered negotiation is presupposed by the political ethics of both traditions. Without that, we should simply revert to the ghetto ethics from which Ramadan is seeking to liberate his co-religionists.[8]

For this reason a Muslim (as well as the practitioner of any other religion) will have a dual or multiple (sometimes called a 'hybrid') identity. This means that there will inevitably be a degree of 'political plurality' where our 'social identities are not constituted by one exclusive set of relations or mode of belonging'.[9] Muslim identity, like all other identities, will be based on a complex set of negotiations.[10]

According to Williams, there are two related dangers which might emerge if a dialogue with Islam is not attempted. On the one hand, he suggests, failure to engage with Muslim groups might lead to the growth of those religious factions who see any participation in the political process as a kind of betrayal. On the other hand, however, ignoring the public and political identity of Islam might strengthen those who regard the secular Government as solely responsible for the construction of public identity. Both might lead to a ghettoisation. Understanding the complex relationships between religious groups and legal and state authority is thus crucial. For this reason the law of the land needs to be clear about precisely what counts as a matter of religious conscience, which brings with it important issues concerning the social and economic status of minority communities and their access to the political process.

This leads Williams on to the problem first, of the place of 'religious scruple' in legal cases, which requires a sensitivity to the religious and cultural 'construction of people's identities'. It becomes imperative that there is some way of distinguishing between cultural habits and 'seriously-rooted matters of faith and discipline'. If there were to be more latitude given to 'rights and scruples rooted in religious identity' there would also need to be an enhanced Muslim legal council to interpret and decide in such matters. Secondly, and more controversially, Williams moves on to discuss the area of 'supplementary jurisdiction' and its relationship with the universal law of the land. He is clear that there needs to be a way of safeguarding and regulating the use of an alternative form of solving legal disputes so that it does not become a way of simply 'reinforcing in minority communities some of the most repressive and retrograde elements in them'. In a plural society there can be no question of taking away rights that are acknowledged as universally valid, or denying any citizen equal access to the law.

Recognising a supplementary jurisdiction, he writes, 'cannot mean recognising a liberty to exert a sort of local monopoly in some areas'. Political plurality consequently means that citizenship will consist of a complex set of sometimes competing identities. Quoting a Jewish legal theorist, he suggests that we need to 'work to overcome the ultimatum of "either your culture or your rights"'.

Williams' third problem concerns the commitment to legal monopoly which is firmly established in European legal systems. While this is central to issues of protection and equality of access to the law, at the same time it fails adequately to grasp the complexities of 'multiple affiliation'. The key point here is the confusion that arises from seeing law as a protection for the citizen as somehow implying that the sovereign state authority has the responsibility for permitting all other levels of identity to exist. Religion would then be a secondary association, or even a purely private matter. Politically this is dangerous principally because it leads to a ghettoised form of social life – religion, which for many is far more than a set of private beliefs and which is key to human identity, would nevertheless be lived out behind closed doors and beyond the reach of the state law. In the pluralist state, according to Williams, law should protect all citizens and consequently monitor the rules and activities which members of all constituent associations – including religious communities – use to regulate their affairs. This is a crucial point in that it prevents the creation of 'mutually isolated communities' where individuals are constrained purely by their communities and traditions and where there can be no public redress.

Law consequently functions as a kind of regulatory framework, 'a way of honouring what in the human constitution is not captured by any one form of corporate belonging or any particular history'. Put simply, in a pluralist context, religion is not a private activity but is a complex

political identity that lives in an uneasy symbiotic relationship with the wider society. This makes George Carey's
criticism of Williams' lecture in *The News of the World*
particularly misguided. He writes that Williams' 'conclusion
that Britain will have to concede some place in law for
aspects of Sharia is a view I cannot share'.[11] But when he
claims that '[t]here can be no exceptions to the laws of our
land which have been so painfully honed by the struggle for
democracy and human rights', one wonders how he would
feel if the Church of England were suddenly forced to accept
equal rights legislation in relation to practising homosexuals
who might be appointed to the episcopate.

Williams' acknowledgement of the need to recognise
the political nature of religious communities which
expresses itself in alternative legal institutions leads him
towards some tentative conclusions: the essentially liberat-
ing vision of universal human rights, he claims, is not
imperilled by a loosening of its monopolistic framework.
Instead in complex plural societies there is a need for
'transformative accommodation' where in carefully circumscribed matters 'power-holders are forced to compete
for the loyalty of their shared constituents'. This system will
be complex and fraught with difficulties. But an over-rigid
application of a monopolistic framework is worse. It can
have the effect of 'ghettoising and effectively disenfranchis-
ing a minority: both jurisdictional parties may be changed
by their encounter over time, and we avoid the sterility of
mutually exclusive monopolies'. While many secularists
find it hard to defend faith schools,[12] Williams suggests that
they 'bring communal loyalties into direct relation with the
wider society and inevitably lead to mutual questioning
and sometimes mutual influence towards change, without
compromising the distinctiveness of the essential elements
of those communal loyalties'.[13] Elsewhere he writes:

To pick up a currently controversial issue, the state's

assistance to 'faith schools' is not the subsidising of exclusivism but the bringing of communities out of isolation to engage with the process of maintaining what they and other communities together need, and to argue and negotiate. The state is thus more than a tribunal; it exercises its lawful character by promoting and resourcing collaboration.[14]

This may well be close to what Tony Blair had in mind in his promotion of Government-funded faith-based schools in one of his final speeches as Prime Minister.[15] The compromises required by access to Government funds would limit fanaticism, and promote tolerance since, as he put it optimistically, 'religious bigotry is inconsistent with most true religion'.

The way forward: interactive pluralism and multiculturalism

What I hope I have shown in the last two chapters is that Williams' long-term project of interactive pluralism is a coherent if controversial approach to politics, which is directly related to multiculturalism and the state's relationship to minority religious communities, which includes the Christian churches. It is rooted in a theological understanding of sovereignty as well as in the equality of all people as created in the image of God. At the same time it draws on a relatively neglected tradition of English political thought which reached its heyday in Edwardian England, but which declined rapidly after the First World War.[16] Interactive pluralism rests on several basic assumptions: first, religion is not a private matter. Even though belonging to a religious community is voluntary and a matter of choice, it nevertheless brings with it a public set of obligations. The religious community is a 'first-level' association which is central for the formation of the political and social identity of its adherents. To treat it as a private matter is to misread the nature of religious belonging. Secondly, although religious adherents will also share other identities, one of which is likely to be national citizenship, the state itself cannot function as a 'first-level' association, at least for religious people. This would be to impose a kind of national and state-directed pseudo-religious homogeneity which would be to overstep the limited nature of sovereignty. Instead the state provides a forum for the negotiation of space, protects the vulnerable, and encourages dialogue, without determining the content and character of that dialogue, nor the precise details of the teachings of the 'first-level associations'.[17] It lives in an often difficult symbiotic relationship with these other political associations.

According to Williams, this means that religions and other social groups do not occupy a 'neutral' and private space, but instead they are political associations.[18] This differentiates him from those liberal multiculturalists who have been criticised by Trevor Phillips who spoke of 'marooned communities ... no-go areas and chronic conflict'.[19] But Williams does not resort to the wishful thinking of those such as Ian Bradley who would create an imaginary community of belonging or a new multi-faith conception of Britishness.[20] Instead, on the basis of his pluralism, Williams identifies a common core of national identity in something far more modest. Belonging to Britain means little more than agreeing to abide by a minimum set of rules for negotiation provided by the space-making state.

The political philosopher Chandran Kukathas has called this sort of pluralist model the 'liberal archipelago'. He defines this as 'a society of societies which is neither the creation nor the object of control of any single authority, though it is a form of order in which authorities function under laws which are themselves beyond the reach of any singular power' (and which consequently have to be settled by negotiation).[21] Under this model, the state is 'no more than a transitory political settlement whose virtue is that it secures civility'.[22] This points in quite the opposite direction from Gordon Brown's efforts to uphold the British ideal. Rather than promoting unity, the state will have little interest in 'cultural integration' or 'cultural engineering', but will be concerned first and foremost with the freedom of association, that is, with providing the conditions for the existence of 'first-level' free associations. Although Williams would probably not go as far as Kukathas, there is nevertheless something important in the claim that 'a liberal society will be one in which politics is given priority over morality'.[23] In such a society the 'state would be a much diminished entity, a good deal less capable of establishing and imposing common standards for the nation'.[24] Morality, we might add, will be developed in the process of negotiation between living communities.

In order that this sort of minimal state might flourish, Williams recognises the need for a participatory form of democracy to ensure that members of the different first-level associations are able to accept the rights and place of other groups, that is, to accept the shared space for negotiation. If this does not happen – which is highly probable when religion is treated by the state simply as private and personal – the likelihood is that ghettoisation will result and there will be little interest in the political process (and little engagement with other 'first-level' associations). Multiculturalism is thus not about fragmentary and competing private goods and the resulting separatism between communities, but instead is about negotiation between different and sometimes competing public truths, between what Modood calls different expressions of a 'sense of groupness' which embrace cultural and religious identities.[25] This negotiation or 'remaking of public identities'[26] takes place, however, within the parameters of certain agreed rules maintained by the law and institutions of the state. Here there is some continuity between Williams and what Anthony Giddens calls 'sophisticated multicultural-ism'.[27] This is the sort of multicultural theory espoused, for instance, by Charles Taylor who stresses the need for mutual recognition and respect between communities within a 'community of fate', that is, within the accidental bound-aries of the national community which makes few meta-physical claims.[28]

What is different for Williams, however, is the priority that he gives to 'first-level associations' rather than to the 'community of fate' (which can sometimes itself become a quasi-structural community, as is the case when it is con-torted into the fixation on 'being British' as a solution to multiple identities). Although much recent Government thinking has focused on community cohesion, on helping groups to negotiate and communicate with one another, there has been rather less emphasis on developing a politi-cal system where negotiation can be promoted without some sort of externally imposed identity (Islam, Asian etc.) as a substitute for a set of voluntary communities of associ-ation (which may be multiple and hybrid). For this to hap-pen in the British context there would need to be major constitutional changes, which would mean serious moves towards decentralisation (as I have suggested earlier in this book).

Despite community cohesion policies, however, par-ticipation in the political process, especially at local levels, has sunk to an all-time low – and that might be because people identify not primarily with the monopolistic legal-istic state (with Britain or Britishness or even England, Wales or Scotland), but with a range of different and far more local groups. For religious people the most important such group is likely to be the community of faith (which may be inseparable from other community affiliations). Since identity is primarily a local business, this means that policies of local enfranchisement and 'inclusion' might be the best starting blocks for the development of a politics of interactive pluralism. In his Chatham lecture, Williams makes some tentative suggestions for how this might affect public policy. Drawing on the work of the Muslim legal theorist, Maleiha Malik, he claims that there

> needs to be a pathway for minority communities to find new ways of identifying with public processes and social institutions, so that (instead of making the main form of protection against discrimination the guarantees provided by the courts, and so consuming immense energy in litigation) specific groups may play a positive role in framing policy before legislation is finalised. And this needs more developed representative institutions of consultation. The issue of 'rights' for a minority religious community thus comes to be allied with a wider set of questions about local democracy and the weaknesses of an 'elective dictatorship' model of parliamentary rule.[29]

Interactive pluralism might well be the best way forward for a healthy democratic state. Politics becomes a negotiation between groups, and in turn the state and its legal system become an arbitrator which favours no one group but which encourages all to contribute and to participate by redirecting decision-making away to the local.

Although this may be too much for many Christians to bear, especially those who long romantically for the harmony of the Christian state, it seems to me to be central for the survival of democracy – and it is far better to learn to live with reality than to cling on to some imaginary past (or, which is even worse, to accept the secularist privatisation of religion). Williams writes:

> ultimately we do not have to be bound by the mythology of purely private conviction and public neutrality;

and, if my general argument is right, the future of religious communities in modern society should show us some ways forward that do not deliver us either into theocracy or into an entirely naked public space.[30]

At the very least interactive pluralism seems a model for political participation which avoids these errors, and for that reason alone it is worth trying. It might also help religions overcome their mutual distrust, suspicion and prejudice. But that requires a humility which only some are able to tolerate. In the concluding chapter I shall explore some of the implications of interactive pluralism for the future of British politics.

CHAPTER SEVEN

Conclusion

This book has sought to explain the crucial importance of 'doing God' in modern British politics. This is not primarily because most people are religious: Chapter 1 showed that they are not. But this misses the point. The old religious consensus of England, and to a lesser extent of Britain, which Matthew Grimley has plausibly shown as lasting at least until the 1960s, was a form of benign political religion where religious and secular values shared much the same space. 'Liberal Anglicanism', he writes, 'provided a theoretical underpinning for English civil religion. It offered a providentialist account of national history and destiny, an organic community, and a religiously sanctioned code of civic obligation.'[1] When shorn of this form of religious underpinning, however, which seems to be what has happened since the 1960s,[2] secularism has little space for alternative forms of political religion. Indeed, in general liberal theories of the state have seen religion as a private phenomenon and a matter of free choice.

Yet – as so many recent events have shown – contemporary expressions of religion are very far from purely private affairs. Chapter 1 showed that significant numbers of people are religious in a way that requires the political and public dimension of religion to be acknowledged. For many practitioners of religion, it simply won't be privatised – indeed this might explain the vociferousness of the militant atheist critiques led by Richard Dawkins[3] and Christopher Hitchens[4] who do not seem able to grasp the contemporary political and social impact of religion after so many years of passive support of the *status quo* by the national religion. Modern religion – especially the religion of many of the recent immigrants to western Europe – simply refuses to conform to the liberal secular model. In their different ways many of the politicians and commentators discussed through the course of this book have recognised this fact, and many have sought to understand the nature of contemporary religion as a public phenomenon. Commentators on both left and right see the central importance of religious dialogue for the problem of community cohesion. As the recent setting up of the Tony Blair Foundation demonstrates, many see inter-religious dialogue as the panacea for many of the failings of modern society.

Yet what seems to me to be lacking in the thinking and policies of most politicians is a recognition that a practical solution to the problems of a lack of social cohesion cannot be addressed without a root-and-branch reform of the political system. The solution to public and political religion cannot be achieved religiously and theologically but only publicly and politically. Participatory pluralist democracy would require a sense of autonomy and responsibility to be returned to local communities. Unless this is recognised then political religion is likely to become separatist and ghettoised. Its adherents will see little point in investing in the wider structures of society. Where political participation makes little practical difference to the form and structure of Government, people will instead seek to determine their own fate within the clearly demarcated boundaries of their own communities. While official community cohesion policies have sought to create more forums for local participation and decision-making, few serious powers in policy formation have been devolved away from the centre. As Chapter 4 showed, Government policy is strong on rhetoric but short on serious redirection of power. Inclusion and participation of all groups in the political process would require more space for negotiation between central and local, but more crucially, a level of commitment to and trust in local democracy. But this is highly unlikely since it steadily declined in importance through most of the twentieth century, and this process accelerated rapidly under Mrs Thatcher with the abolition of metropolitan counties and the removal of many of the powers from local authorities.

There is consequently a very long way to go. This is despite some of the rhetoric of devolution and acknowledging that in some parts of the country there have been significant powers released by Westminster. Where local democracy is little more than an elected provider of centrally driven services, the idea of autonomy and significant decision-making is completely absent. Again, it seems to me that a complete rethink of the relationship between the centre and the local is crucial – the decline of voter participation, especially in local politics, is hardly surprising when local government is simply a deliverer of centrally set and regulated targets. A central focus of Blair's third term, which has continued under Gordon Brown, has been to regard citizens increasingly as consumers (i.e. passive users) of education, health, and other public services which deliver centrally imposed objectives and which seek to achieve 'national' targets. Citizens 'choose' between competing services. This means that they cannot be participating agents and decision-makers in policy-creation and delivery, any more than they could be responsible for the design and delivery of a new model of car or washing powder. Community cohesion is unlikely to be effective, at least in relation to political participation, unless there is a reorientation of political decision-making and a move away from target-driven consumerism.

Without this reversal in the political process, however, there seems little hope of the reinvigoration of democracy (and communities) either at a local or national level. As I have suggested, there are some signs for hope that a policy of reinvigorated local democracy might be established – devolution in Scotland, Wales and London for instance, has at least questioned the centrally driven policy objectives of the Westminster system. Minority government in Scotland has forced coalition building and consensus politics through negotiation. There is also much in the recent policy statements that speaks of devolution and a decentralization of power away from the centre to the local. There is also frequent recognition of the need for participation in local structures of government.

However, in England at least, the central regulative framework is as tight as ever. 'Post-democracy', as Colin Crouch calls it, is a situation that needs to be addressed through the creation of more flexible and responsive institutions entrusted with far greater responsibility for setting policy objectives and delivery.[5] Only in this way will those affected by policies feel they have a stake in politics. However, as Tom Bentley writes: 'There is little sign that the new infrastructure of regulation, procurement and implementation is able to offer the forms of responsiveness or local legitimacy that such approaches have been seeking, even when their political champions are passionately committed to creating them.'[6] The idea of local legitimacy is key to the success of community cohesion. And this has little to do with shared British values, or unity in diversity, but far more to do with trust in the rough and tumble of democratic negotiation at the local level. This is likely to be messy and there will be constant squabbles and conflicts, but there will also have to be compromises imposed by the need to live together and to share the same space.

The question that emerges for members of religious communities is simple. How far can these institutions of democracy be reshaped to encourage participation without homogenisation or simple assimilation? Here it is worth mentioning the recent wide-ranging (and glossy) Church of England and Methodist Report, *Faithful Cities*. This report has drawn a great deal on the community cohesion literature and has even developed the notion of 'faithful capital' as a religious equivalent to 'social capital', based on shared values underpinned by religious practice and beliefs.[7] The Report celebrates diversity and co-operation between communities, and has many practical examples of successful community work by the churches. It also offers impressive reflection on the changing nature of public and private,[8] as well as the lack of serious local input in decision-making.[9] While recognising the democratic deficit, it does not address solutions in any detail. Instead it looks at the role of the churches in delivering services and promoting diversity and cohesion. However, it recognises some of the problems that would emerge from increasing involvement of the so-called Third Sector in policy delivery. It is easy for churches and other voluntary organisations to become deliverers of a centrally set policy to consumers of services with little sense of participation in the formulation of that policy (or indeed possibility of critique of those policies).[10] The Third Sector would be as equally unparticipatory as the traditional providers of services, and would still be at the beck and call of central Government targets, 'with the Church simply accepting the Government proscriptions and prescriptions in order to be in partnership'. The Report goes on:

> When government holds all the cards it has a 'structural

advantage'. It may offer rewards, for example, in the shape of funding to carry out a project, or offer inclusion such as with a seat at the (planning) table. But this may be the equivalent of being co-opted, and being co-opted undermines the ability to critique what is going on. Such a power play is subverted if the Church refuses the blandishments of co-option and, instead, models the way of Jesus and lives with the vulnerable, the weak and the excluded.[11]

This is an important point. Where local authorities have been effectively depoliticised, it becomes important for churches to retain a critical detachment. Indeed, it may well be that less time and expense should be devoted by churches to policy delivery, and more energy should be put into reinvigorating the witness of Christians in the democratic process and in voluntary organisations: that, after all, tends to be where Christians have traditionally made the greatest impact. This would mean that the role of the Church is more about inspiring its members with Gospel values to live and work in the power of the Spirit in the world rather than becoming simply another agency or pressure group.[12]

Finally, and this is my most important point, it may simply be impossible, except in a very vague and ultimately pointless way, to find any mutually shared universal values. A situation which so clearly emerged in the great European Wars of Religion in the sixteenth and seventeenth centuries has returned. While many communities claim universality and a vision of truth which would encompass all others, the very fact of plurality forces a degree of co-existence. All those who wish to share the same space are required to think seriously about the nature of truth and how it can co-exist with other interpretations and visions. One solution is to locate the interpretation of public truth in the state – this amounts to the secular solution which has most obviously been adopted in France. But this requires a redefinition of religion as a private matter which few adherents would wish to adopt.

Another solution is a sort of federation of religious communities happily trying to live with one another. But this, it seems to me, is impossible. Firstly – and obviously – most religious communities have enough problems trying to live together among themselves. Among Christians, conflict has been the normal condition of churches throughout most of history, and the recent history of my own Anglican Communion is a good case study in conflict-management and aggressive posturing. Secondly, if identities are complex, and if the understanding of culture (like religion and ethnicity) is bitterly contested, then the idea of a federation of different religious (or ethnic) communities is both implausible and possibly dangerous – who, after all, will ultimately decide which categories people will fall under? This is one of the reasons why some critics of multiculturalism, including Trevor Phillips, have used such powerful rhetoric.[13] Pluralism as an alternative solution is a form of pragmatic regulation which requires a degree of consent to a shared minimum for co-existence.

Another alternative is that of strong national communities based on historical myths, which has been one popular option in recent years – the idea of Britain, according to Gordon Brown, might provide a set of universalist and inclusive values that would serve as a remedy to fragmentation. However, this solution seems to me to be at the very least risky, and could be seen as an attempt to homogenise society and deny the vitality of minorities (as has happened at times in polarised societies such as Sri Lanka). Virtually all the examples one can cite of British (or more usually English) values are ambiguous. They have excluded as well as included. The imperial and post-colonial legacy makes a new revived sense of Britishness highly complex. The combinations required in a new British identity can easily stretch things beyond credibility – this can be highlighted in such strange and ambiguous images as Pakistani taxi drivers in Bradford flying the crusaders' flag of St George during the 2004 World Cup.[14]

The fourth option is outlined above in Chapters 5 and 6. 'Interactive pluralism', as developed in relation to multi-culturalism by Rowan Williams, offers a straightforward and pragmatic solution to the problem of public religion in a modern state. Here I think there is much of interest in Anthony Giddens's idea of what he calls 'sophisticated' as opposed to 'naïve' multiculturalism which resists simple categorisation of ethnic and religious identity, but which allows for a plurality of identities to co-exist on the basis of Government-promoted mutual respect. The minimum rules are laid down for negotiations to happen, but there is little sense in which the state itself provides a core of cultural identity. Many will no doubt choose to regard themselves simply as British or English or Welsh or Scottish, and identify with the dominant historical myths and traditions. But many will choose not to do so, and will hold more complex identities which depend on a whole range of ethnic and religious factors. What is key is that the state provides structures whereby these different identities can be held together.[15] Indeed, working out the necessary pragmatic principles for such a society to function seems to me to be the key role for Government.

This means that the principal issue in modern multi-cultural politics is less that of finding shared values than that of providing structures so that people can learn to live with others who are in some ways different but also in some ways the same. This is what might be referred to as a form of 'patriotism' which amounts to little more than a commitment to respect one another and to negotiate with one another despite cultural and religious differences.[16] This, I think, is the cash value of much of the talk about Britishness and citizenship. The minimum requirement is to let others co-exist, even when we might disagree profoundly, provided that there is a mutuality of respect. In order for such a policy to work, it might at times be necessary for Government action to restrain those who clamour for singular identity at the expense of others (including fundamentalists). Going much further, however, and providing too many positive values (of, say, Britishness) seems both pointless and unnecessarily conflictual, especially for those whose historical identity is based on not being 'British' in that way. Indeed, the traditional marks of Britishness, not least the Union Flag, may be highly controversial as unifying symbols. Besides, few people like to be told what values they should adopt by central Government, or indeed that they have a duty to integrate at all. What Giddens imagines instead is what he calls 'acceptance of a common overall identity as members of a national community, as a "community of fate" – that is, being bound by laws and collective decisions that affect everyone'.[17] That may well be what citizenship – another recent concept in British politics – is really about. Britain (and any other country for that matter) is where people happen to live and it is best for them if they learn to live together with one another in relative peace and tranquillity. And I would want to add that feeling at home is best achieved through participation in a decision-making process.

A degree of value pluralism is inevitable, in which case it might be better to return to tolerant multiculturalism rather than to impose a centrally determined idea of what counts as a good community. Rather than sponsoring 'community cohesion', the British Government (and the same could be said of other governments) might be well advised to expend energy on working out the limits of pluralism through promoting the language of rights and equality, without worrying too much about corresponding responsibilities and duties or the promotion of community. At the same time, it needs to sacrifice power for the sake of participation. Contemporary identities might simply be too confusing for governments to understand – and popular politics, with its tendency to media simplification, can easily create forms of exclusive identity with violent repercussions. Ultimately equality before the law, and equality of access and opportunity for all people, whatever their identities, may be far more important than community cohesion. And we can then leave community cohesion to what has been called the 'weak social capital' of democratic governance based on coming together to make decisions in a whole range of groups underpinned by strong local government.[18] The choice for governments is either to dictate the terms of the debate, or to let people dictate the terms for themselves. And for those of us who do not live in Westminster, we will need to do this at the coal-face – that is, where we live and engage with others. It is also where religious people express their faith publicly. The panacea for the problems of community cohesion lies in trusting the people. As R. H. Tawney once said: it is 'the condition … of freedom that men should not be ruled by an authority which they cannot control'.[19] But strong executives tend not to like to lose control, and they usually seem to think that they know best. In the end, this might be disastrous for a flourishing state.

BIBLIOGRAPHY[1]

Archbishop of Canterbury's Commission on Urban Priority Areas, *Faith in the City: A Call for Action by Church and Nation* (London, Church House Publishing, 1985)

Jacinta Ashworth and Ian Farthing, *Churchgoing in the UK: A research report from Tearfund on church attendance in the UK* (London, Tearfund, April 2007)

Arthur Aughey, *The Politics of Englishness* (Manchester, Manchester University Press, 2007)

Paul Avis, *Anglicanism and the Christian Church* (London, T. & T. Clark, 2002)

Paul Bagguley and Yasmin Hussain, 'Conflict and Cohesion: constructions of "community" around the 2001 "riots"' (lecture to 2003 Communities Conference) at: http://www.leeds.ac.uk/sociology/people/pbdocs/Conflict%20and%20Cohesion%204%20conference.doc

Paul Bagguley and Yasmin Hussain, 'Flying the Flag for England? Citizenship, Religion and Cultural Identity among British Pakistani Muslims' in Tahir Abbas (ed.), *Muslim Britain: Communities under Pressure* (London, Zed Books, 2005), pp. 222–33

Zygmunt Bauman, 'Britain after Blair, or Thatcherism Consolidated' in Hassan (ed.), *After Blair*, pp. 60–74

David Bebbington, *The Mind of Gladstone: Religion, Homer, and Politics* (Oxford, Oxford University Press, 2004)

Tom Bentley, 'Learning to let go: The potential of a self-creating society' in Hassan (ed.), *After Blair*, pp. 94–106

Welmoet Boender and Meryem Kanmaz, 'Imams in the Netherlands and Islam Teachers in Flanders' in Wasf Shadid and Sjoerd van Koningsveld (eds.), *Intercultural Relations and Religious Authorities: Muslims in the European Union* (Leuven, Peeters, 2002), pp. 169–80

Pierre Bourdieu, 'Cultural Reproduction and Social Reproduction', in J. Karabel and A. H. Halsey (eds.), *Power and Ideology in Education* (Oxford, Oxford University Press, 1977), pp. 487–511

Ian Bradley, *Believing in Britain* (London, I. B. Tauris, 2007)

Andrew Bradstock, *Louder than Words: Action for the 21st-century Church* (London, DLT, 2007)

Peter Brierley, *Religious Trends No. 1: 1999/2000* (London, Christian Research, 1999)

Callum Brown, *The People in the Pews: Religion and Society in Scotland since 1780* (Glasgow, Economic and Social History of Scotland, 1993)

Callum Brown, *The Death of Christian Britain* (London, Routledge, 2001)

Callum Brown, '"Best not to take it too far": how the British cut religion down to size' at: http://www.opendemocracy.net/globalization-aboutfaith/britain_religion_3335.jsp

Callum Brown, *Religion and Society in Twentieth-Century Britain* (Harlow, Pearson Longman, 2006)

Christopher G. A. Bryant, *The Nations of Britain* (Oxford, Oxford University Press, 2006)

Gordon Brown, 'State and Market: Towards a Public Interest Test' in *Political Quarterly* 74 (2003), pp. 266–84

Gordon Brown, 'Britishness' (7 July 2004) in *Moving Britain Forward: Selected Speeches 1997–2006* (London, Bloomsbury, 2006), pp. 1–26

Steve Bruce, *Religion in Modern Britain* (Oxford, Oxford University Press, 1995)

Steve Bruce, *God is Dead: Secularization in the West* (Oxford, Blackwell, 2002)

J. W. Burrow, 'The Village Community' in Neil McKendrick (ed.), *Historical Perspectives: Studies in English Thought and Society* (London, Europa, 1974), pp. 255–84

Alex Callinicos, *Against the Third Way* (Cambridge, Polity Press, 2001)

Helen Cameron, 'Decline of the Church in England' in Grace Davie, Paul Heelas and Linda Woodhead (eds.), *Predicting Religion* (Aldershot, Ashgate, 2003), pp. 109–19

Ted Cantle, *Community Cohesion: A Report of the Independent Review Team Chaired by Ted Cantle* (London, Home Office, 2001)

Ted Cantle, *Community Cohesion: A New Framework for Race and Diversity* (Basingstoke, Palgrave, 2005)

José Casanova, *Public Religions in the Modern World* (Chicago, Chicago University Press, 1994)

Paul Chambers, 'Contentious Headscarves: Spirituality and the State in the Twenty-First Century' in Kieran Flanagan and Peter C. Jupp (eds.), *The Sociology of Spirituality* (Aldershot, Ashgate, 2007), pp. 127–43

Mark D. Chapman, *Blair's Britain* (London, DLT, 2005)

Mark D. Chapman, 'Theology in the Public Arena: The Case of English Bonhoefferism' in Jane Garnett, Matthew Grimley, Alana Harris, William Whyte and Sarah Williams (eds.), *Redefining Christian*

Britain: Post 1945 Perspectives (London, SCM Press, 2007), pp. 92–105

Mark D. Chapman, *Bishops, Saints and Politics* (London, T. & T. Clark, 2007)

Mark D. Chapman, 'The Dull Bits of History: Cautionary Tales for Anglicanism' in Mark D. Chapman (ed.), *The Anglican Covenant: Unity and Diversity in the Anglican Communion* (London, Mowbray, 2008), pp. 81–99

Anthony Clarke, *Burnley Task Force Report* (Burnley, Burnley Task Force, 2001)

G. D. H. Cole, *Socialism and Fascism, 1931–1939* (A History of Socialist Thought, Vol. V) (New York, St Martin's Press, 1960)

Linda Colley, *Britons: Forging the Nation, 1707–1837* (New Haven, Yale University Press, 1992)

Robert Colls, *Identity of England* (Oxford, Oxford University Press, 2002)

Commission on Urban Life and Faith, *Faithful Cities: A Call for Celebration, Vision and Justice* (London, Church House Publishing and Peterborough, Methodist Publishing House, 2006)

Colin Crouch, *Post-Democracy* (Cambridge, Polity, 2004)

Grace Davie, *Religion in Britain since 1945: Believing without Belonging* (Oxford, Blackwell, 1994)

Grace Davie, *Religion in Modern Europe: A Memory Mutates* (Oxford, Oxford University Press, 2000)

Grace Davie, *Europe: The Exceptional Case: Parameters of Faith in the Modern World* (London, DLT, 2002)

Grace Davie, *Sociology of Religion* (London, Sage, 2007)

Norman Davies, *The Isles: A History* (London, Macmillan, 1999)

Richard Dawkins, *The God Delusion* (London, Black Swan, 2007)

John Denham, *Building Cohesive Communities: A Report of the Ministerial Group on Public Order and Community Cohesion* (London, Home Office, 2001)

Émile Durkheim, *The Division of Labour in Society* (1893); English translation (Glencoe, Illinois, The Free Press, 1947)

Émile Durkheim, *The Elementary Forms of the Religious Life* (1912); English translation (London, George Allen and Unwin, 1915)

Edward A. Freeman, *The Growth of the Constitution* (London, Macmillan, 3rd edn, 1876)

Doug Gay, 'Faith in, with and under Gordon Brown: A Scottish Presbyterian/Calvinist Reflection' in *International Journal of Public Theology* 1 (2007), pp. 306–20

Doug Gay, 'From the Vicar of St Albans to the Minister of Alba – A Scottish Presbyterian Reading of Gordon Brown' in *Third Way* (forthcoming).

Sharif Gemie, 'Stasi's Republic: the school and the "veil", December

2003–March 2004' in *Modern and Contemporary France* 12 (2006), pp. 387–97

Anthony Giddens, *Over to You, Mr Brown* (Cambridge, Polity, 2007) p. 155

Robin Gill, 'Religion in Twentieth-century Kent' in Nigel Yates (ed.), *Kent in the Twentieth Century* (Woodbridge, Boydell, 2001)

Sue Goss, 'Re-imagining the public realm' in Hassan (ed.), *After Blair*, pp. 107–19

Ron Greaves, 'Negotiating British Citizenship and Muslim Identity' in Tahir Abbas (ed.), *Muslim Britain: Communities under Pressure* (London, Zed Books, 2005), pp. 66–77

Matthew Grimley, *Citizenship, Community, and the Church of England: Liberal Anglican Theories of the State Between the Wars* (Oxford, Clarendon Press, 2004)

Gerry Hassan (ed.), *After Blair: Politics after the New Labour Decade* (London, Lawrence and Wishart, 2007)

Paul Heelas and Linda Woodhead, *The Spiritual Revolution: Why religion is giving way to spirituality* (Oxford, Blackwell, 2005)

Simon Heffer, *Nor Shall my Sword: The Reinvention of England* (London, Weidenfeld and Nicolson, 1999)

Peter Hinchliff, *God and History* (Oxford, Clarendon, 1992)

Christopher Hitchens, *God is not Great: How Religion Poisons Everything* (New York, Atlantic, 2008)

Samuel P. Huntington, *The Clash of Civilizations and the Remaking of World Order* (New York, Simon and Schuster, 1996)

Philip Jenkins, *God's Continent: Christianity, Islam, and Europe's Religious Crisis* (New York, Oxford University Press, 2007)

Hannah Jones, 'Faith in Community', *eSharp* Issue 7, pp. 11–13 at: http://www.sharp.arts.gla.ac. uk/issue7/Jones.pdf

Michael Keith, *Riots, Race and Policing: Lore and Disorder in a Multi-Racial Society* (London, UCL Press, 1993)

Anthony King, *The British Constitution* (Oxford, Oxford University Press, 2007)

Chandran Kukathas, *The Liberal Archipelago: A Theory of Diversity and Freedom* (Oxford, Oxford University Press, 2003)

Harold Laski, *Political Thought in England from Locke to Bentham* (London, Williams and Norgate, 1920)

Simon Lee, *Best for Britain: The Politics and Legacy of Gordon Brown* (Oxford, Oneworld, 2007)

Stanford M. Lyman, 'The Gothic Foundation of Robert E. Park's conception of race and culture' in Luigi Tomasi (ed.), *The Tradition of the Chicago School of Sociology* (Aldershot, Ashgate, 1998)

Derek McGhee, 'Moving to "our" common ground –a critical examination of community cohesion discourse in twenty-first century

Britain' in *The Sociological Review* 51 (2003), pp. 376–404

Donald MacKinnon, 'Kenosis and Establishment' in *The Stripping of the Altars* (London, Fontana, 1969), pp. 13–40

Iain McLean, *Adam Smith: Radical and Egalitarian: An Interpretation for the Twenty-first Century* (Edinburgh, Edinburgh University Press, 2006)

Hugh McLeod, *Religion and Society in England, 1850–1914* (London, Macmillan, 1996)

Hugh McLeod, *The Religious Crisis of the 1960s* (Oxford, Oxford University Press, 2007)

Henry Maine, *Village Communities in the East and West* (London, John Murray, 1890)

Maleiha Malik, 'Muslims and Participatory Democracy', in Mohammad Siddique Seddon, Dilwar Hussain and Nadeem Malik (eds.), *British Muslims: Loyalty and Belonging* (Islamic Foundation, London, Citizen Organising Foundation, 2003), pp. 69–85

Frederick Medis (ed.), *The Church of Ceylon: A History 1945–1995* (Colombo, Diocese of Ceylon, 1995)

P. A. Mellor and C. Shilling, *Re-forming the Body: Religion, Community and Modernity* (London, Sage, 1997)

John Milbank, *Theology and Social Theory* (Oxford, Blackwell, 1990)

Tariq Modood, 'Reflections on the Rushdie Affair: Muslims, Race and Equality in Britain' in *Multicultural Politics*, pp. 103–12

Tariq Modood, 'Multiculturalism, Secularism, and the State', in *Multicultural Politics*, pp. 131–50

Tariq Modood, *Multicultural Politics: Racism, Ethnicity and Muslims in Britain* (Edinburgh, Edinburgh University Press, 2007)

Tariq Modood, *Multiculturalism: A Civic Idea* (Cambridge, Polity, 2007)

Tom Nairn, *The Break-up of Britain* (London, NLB, 1977)

Tom Nairn, *After Britain* (London, Granta, 2000)

New Local Government Network, *Towards a New Localism* (London, NLGN, 2000)

David Nicholls, 'Authority in Church and State aspects of the thought of J. N. Figgis and his contemporaries' (unpublished Cambridge PhD diss., 1962)

David Nicholls, *The Pluralist State* (London, Macmillan, 2nd edn, 1994)

D. Osborne and T. Gabeler, *Re-inventing Government: How the Entrepreneurial Spirit is Transforming the Public Sector* (Reading, Mass., Addison-Wesley, 1992)

Herman Ouseley, *Community Pride, Not Prejudice: Making Diversity Work in Practice* (Bradford, Bradford Vision, 2001)

Bhikhu Parekh for the Commission for Multi-Ethnic Britain, *The Future of Multi-Ethnic Britain* (London, Profile Books, 2000)

Bhikhu Parekh, *Rethinking Multiculturalism: Cultural Diversity and*

Political Thinking (Basingstoke, Palgrave Macmillan, 2nd edn, 2006)

Christopher Parker, *The English Historical Tradition since 1850* (Edinburgh, John Donald, 1990)

Robert Peston, *Brown's Britain* (London, Short Books, 2006)

A. Pollock, *NHS plc: The Privatisation of our Health Care* (London, Verso, 2005)

Lawrence Pratchett, 'Local Autonomy, Local Democracy and the "New Localism"', in *Political Studies* 52 (2004), pp. 358–75

Frank Prochaska, *Christianity and Social Service in Modern Britain: The Disinherited Spirit* (Oxford, Oxford University Press, 2006)

Robert D. Putnam, *Bowling Alone: The Collapse and Revival of American Community* (New York, Simon and Schuster, 2000)

Tariq Ramadan, *Western Muslims and the Future of Islam* (Oxford, Oxford University Press, 2004)

John Rex, 'Urban Segregation in Great Britain', in Ceri Peach, Vaughan Robinson and Susan Smith (eds.), *Ethnic Segregation in Cities* (London, Croom Helm, 1981), pp. 25–42

David Ritchie, *Oldham Independent Review Panel Report* (Manchester, Government Office for the North-west, 2001)

Paul Routledge, *Gordon Brown* (London, Simon and Schuster, 1998)

Jonathan Sacks, *The Dignity of Difference: How to Avoid the Clash of Civilisations* (London, Continuum, revised edn, 2003)

Roger Scruton, *England: An Elegy* (London, Chatto and Windus, 2000)

Amartya Sen, *Identity and Violence* (London, Allen Lane, 2006)

Marc Stears, *Progressives, Pluralists, and the Problems of the State: Ideologies of Reform in the United States and Britain, 1909–1926* (Oxford, Oxford University Press, 2002)

R. H. Tawney, *The Acquisitive Society* (London, G. Bell, 1921)

Charles Taylor, 'Multiculturalism and "the politics of recognition"'. in A. Gutman (ed.), *Multiculturalism and "the politics of recognition"* (Princeton, Princeton University Press, 1994)

Charles Taylor, *Multiculturalism: Examining the Politics of Recognition* (Princeton, Princeton University Press, 1994)

Jenny Taylor, 'British Government and the Inner Cities' in Grace Davie, Paul Heelas and Linda Woodhead (eds.), *Predicting Religion* (Aldershot, Ashgate, 2003), pp. 120–32

Keith Thomas, *Religion and the Decline of Magic* (London, Penguin, 1973)

Emily Thornberry, Rick Muir and Ian Kearns, 'Power Politics: Who runs Britain?', in Nick Pearce and Julia Margo (eds.), *Politics for a New Generation* (London, Palgrave Macmillan, 2007), pp. 279–302

Tony Travers, 'Local Government' in Anthony Seldon (ed.), *Blair's Britain* (Cambridge, Cambridge University Press, 2007), pp. 54–78

Ferdinand Tönnies, 'The Concept of Gemeinschaft', in Werner J.

Cahnman and Rudolf Heberle (eds.), *Ferdinand Tönnies on Sociology: Pure, Applied and Empirical. Selected Writings* (Chicago, University of Chicago Press, 1971), pp. 62–72

Ferdinand Tönnies, *Community and Civil Society*, translated by José Harris and M. Hollis (Cambridge, Cambridge University Press, 2001)

David Voas and Steve Bruce, 'The Spiritual Revolution: Another False Dawn for the Sacred' in Kieran Flanagan and Peter C. Jupp (eds.), *The Sociology of Spirituality* (Aldershot, Ashgate, 2007), pp. 43–61

Nira Wickramasinghe, *Sri Lanka in the Modern Age: A History of Contested Identities* (Colombo, Vijitha Yapa Publications, 2006)

Rowan Williams, 'What is Catholic Orthodoxy?' in Kenneth Leech and Rowan Williams (eds.), *Essays Catholic and Radical* (London, Bowardean, 1983), pp. 11–25

Rowan Williams, 'Liberation Theology and the Anglican Tradition' in Rowan Williams and David Nicholls (eds.), *Politics and Theological Identity: Two Anglican Essays* (London, The Jubilee Group, 1984), pp. 7–26

Rowan Williams, 'The Incarnation as the Basis for Dogma' in Robert Morgan (ed.), *The Religion of the Incarnation* (Bristol, Bristol Classical Press, 1989), pp. 85–98

Rowan Williams, 'The Trinity and Pluralism' in *On Christian Theology* (Oxford, Blackwell, 2000), pp. 167–80.

NOTES

Chapter 1: On Not Doing God

1. Video at: http://news.bbc.co.uk/1/hi/uk/4208250.stm
2. Samuel P. Huntington, *The Clash of Civilizations and the Remaking of World Order* (New York, Simon and Schuster, 1996).
3. One of the best and most dispassionate accounts of the recent development of Islam in Europe is Philip Jenkins, *God's Continent: Christianity, Islam, and Europe's Religious Crisis* (New York, Oxford University Press, 2007).
4. On this, see David Bebbington, *The Mind of Gladstone: Religion, Homer, and Politics* (Oxford, Oxford University Press, 2004).
5. See Mark D. Chapman, *Blair's Britain* (London, DLT, 2005), pp. 76–82.
6. John Milbank, *Theology and Social Theory* (Oxford, Blackwell, 1990), p. 104.
7. *Daily Telegraph*, 27 November 1997.
8. Doug Gay, 'Faith in, with and under Gordon Brown: A Scottish Presbyterian/Calvinist Reflection' in *International Journal of Public Theology* 1 (2007), pp. 306–20.
9. Doug Gay, 'From the Vicar of St Albans to the Minister of Alba – A Scottish Presbyterian Reading of Gordon Brown' in *Third Way* (forthcoming).
10. *Evening Standard*, 5 March 1993.
11. Cited in Paul Vallely, 'Gordon Brown and the making of a Prime Minister' in *The Independent*, 28 June 2007.
12. Interview with Lynn Barber in *The Daily Telegraph*, 10 July 1995, cited in Paul Routledge, *Gordon Brown* (London, Simon and Schuster, 1998), p. 25.
13. *The Independent*, 20 December 2007.
14. Gordon Brown, speech to the Labour Party Conference, 25 September 2006 at: http://www.guardian.co.uk/politics/2006/sep/25/labourconference.labour2>
15. http://www.labour.org.uk/leadership/gordon_brown_s_leader_of_the_labour_party

16. *The Independent*, 30 May 2006.

17. See Simon Lee, *Best for Britain: The Politics and Legacy of Gordon Brown* (Oxford, Oneworld, 2007), ch. 2.

18. At: http://www.hm-treasury.gov.uk/Newsroom_and_Speeches/speeches/statement/speech_statement_060597.cfm

19. Iain McLean, *Adam Smith: Radical and Egalitarian: An Interpretation for the Twenty-first Century* (Edinburgh, Edinburgh University Press, 2006), pp. 142–3.

20. At: http://news.bbc.co.uk/1/hi/uk/7157409.stm

21. 9 March 2006.

22. See the judgement at: http://www.ofcom.org.uk/tv/obb/prog_cb/obb79/

23. *The Daily Telegraph*, 7 April 1996.

24. *The Times*, 2 May 2003.

25. Transcript at: http://news.bbc.co.uk/2/hi/programmes/newsnight/2732979.stm

26. At: http://tonyblairoffice.org/2007/12/interfaith.html

27. 'Faith and Globalisation', The Cardinal's Lectures 2008, Westminster Cathedral, London, 3 April 2008 at: http://tonyblairoffice.org/2008/04/speech-on-faith-globalisation.html

28. Callum Brown, '"Best not to take it too far": how the British cut religion down to size' at: http://www.opendemocracy.net/globalization-aboutfaith/britain_religion_3335.jsp

29. On this, see, for instance Steve Bruce, *God is Dead: Secularization in the West* (Oxford, Blackwell, 2002), esp. pp. 60–74; and *Religion in Modern Britain* (Oxford, Oxford University Press, 1995).

30. At: http://www.statistics.gov.uk/cci/nugget.asp?id=293

31. Jacinta Ashworth and Ian Farthing, *Churchgoing in the UK: A research report from Tearfund on church attendance in the UK* (London, Tearfund, April 2007) at: http://news.bbc.co.uk/1/shared/bsp/hi/pdfs/03_04_07_tearfundchurch.pdf

32. At: http://www.christian-research.org.uk

33. This is roughly in line with the latest figures from September 2007, where 43 per cent of the 1000 adults surveyed never attended church apart from funerals, baptisms and weddings. See http://www.cofe.anglican.org/info/statistics/orb2007churchpowattendance.pdf

34. At: http://www.churchsurvey.co.uk/?home

35. On this see Grace Davie, *Religion in Modern Europe: A Memory Mutates* (Oxford, Oxford University Press, 2000), esp. ch. 1; and *Europe: The Exceptional Case: Parameters of Faith in the Modern World* (London, DLT, 2002), esp. pp. 6–7.

36. Callum Brown, *The People in the Pews: Religion and Society in Scotland since 1780* (Glasgow, Economic and Social History of

Scotland, 1993), p. 7.

37. Steve Bruce, *God is Dead*, op. cit., p. 63.

38. Figures in Peter Brierley, *Religious Trends No. 1: 1999/2000* (London, Christian Research, 1999).

39. Robin Gill, 'Religion in Twentieth-century Kent' in Nigel Yates (ed.), *Kent in the Twentieth Century* (Woodbridge, Boydell, 2001), pp. 321–33.

40. Callum Brown, *The Death of Christian Britain* (London, Routledge, 2001); and *Religion and Society in Twentieth-Century Britain* (Harlow, Pearson Longman, 2006).

41. Hugh McLeod, *The Religious Crisis of the 1960s* (Oxford, Oxford University Press, 2007).

42. See Paul Heelas and Linda Woodhead, *The Spiritual Revolution: why religion is giving way to spirituality* (Oxford, Blackwell, 2005) and David Voas and Steve Bruce, 'The Spiritual Revolution: Another False Dawn for the Sacred' in Kieran Flanagan and Peter C. Jupp (eds.), *The Sociology of Spirituality* (Aldershot, Ashgate, 2007), pp. 43–61.

43. Helen Cameron, 'Decline of the Church in England' in Grace Davie, Paul Heelas and Linda Woodhead (eds.), *Predicting Religion* (Aldershot, Ashgate, 2003), pp. 109–19, esp. p. 118.

44. Tariq Modood, *Multiculturalism: A Civic Idea* (Cambridge, Polity, 2007), p. 85.

45. José Casanova, *Public Religions in the Modern World* (Chicago, Chicago University Press, 1994).

46. See Paul Chambers, 'Contentious Headscarves: Spirituality and the State in the Twenty-First Century' in Flanagan and Jupp (eds.), *The Sociology of Spirituality*, op. cit., pp. 127–43.

47. Sharif Gemie, 'Stasi's Republic: the school and the "veil", December 2003–March 2004' in *Modern and Contemporary France* 12 (2006), pp. 387–97, here p. 395.

48. P. A. Mellor and C. Shilling, *Re-forming the Body: Religion, Community and Modernity* (London, Sage, 1997).

49. See Modood, *Multiculturalism*, op. cit., pp. 75–8.

50. Tariq Modood, *Multicultural Politics: Racism, Ethnicity and Muslims in Britain* (Edinburgh, Edinburgh University Press, 2007), p. 18.

51. Ibid., p. 140.

Chapter 2: Building Community

1. Mark D. Chapman, *Blair's Britain* (London, DLT, 2005), ch. 3. See also Alex Callinicos, *Against the Third Way* (Cambridge, Polity Press, 2001), esp. pp. 55–67.

2. On this, see Chapman, *Blair's Britain*, op. cit., ch. 6.

3. See Pierre Bourdieu, 'Cultural Reproduction and Social

Reproduction', in J. Karabel and A. H. Halsey (eds.), *Power and Ideology in Education* (Oxford, Oxford University Press, 1977), pp. 487–511.

4. Robert D. Putnam, *Bowling Alone: The Collapse and Revival of American Community* (New York, Simon and Schuster, 2000), p. 19.

5. Ibid., p. 27.

6. Ibid., p. 63.

7. Ibid., p. 19.

8. Ibid., pp. 294–5.

9. Ibid., p. 401.

10. Ibid., pp. 22–4.

11. Zygmunt Bauman, 'Britain after Blair, or Thatcherism Consolidated' in Gerry Hassan (ed.), *After Blair: Politics after the New Labour Decade* (London, Lawrence and Wishart, 2007), pp. 60–74, here p. 61 (author's emphasis).

12. Bauman, 'Britain after Blair', op. cit., p. 65.

13. Ibid., p. 62. Margaret Thatcher made this famous statement in an interview published in *Woman's Own* on 23 September 1987. What she actually said was not quite as individualistic as Bauman and most other critics have thought: 'who is society? There is no such thing! There are individual men and women and there are families and no government can do anything except through people and people look to themselves first. It is our duty to look after ourselves and then also to help look after our neighbour and life is a reciprocal business and people have got the entitlements too much in mind without the obligations.'

14. See J. W. Burrow, 'The Village Community' in Neil McKendrick (ed.), *Historical Perspectives: Studies in English Thought and Society* (London, Europa, 1974), pp. 255–84. Tönnies was strongly influenced by Sir Henry Maine, *Village Communities in the East and West* (London, John Murray, 1890).

15. See, for instance, the classic account by Keith Thomas, *Religion and the Decline of Magic* (London, Penguin, 1973), esp. p. 41.

16. Hugh McLeod has charted the changing nature of community in England in *Religion and Society in England, 1850–1914* (London, Macmillan, 1996).

17. Ferdinand Tönnies, 'The Concept of Gemeinschaft', in Werner J. Cahnman and Rudolf Heberle (eds.), *Ferdinand Tönnies on Sociology: Pure, Applied and Empirical. Selected Writings* (Chicago, University of Chicago Press, 1971), pp. 62–72, here p. 69. See also the new translation by José Harris and M. Hollis of Tönnies' classic work, *Gemeinschaft und Gesellschaft: Community and Civil Society* (Cambridge, Cambridge University Press, 2001).

18. Edward A. Freeman, *The Growth of the Constitution* (London,

Macmillan, 3rd edn, 1876), p. 1. On the idea of Englishness and identity, see Robert Colls' wide-ranging survey in *Identity of England* (Oxford, Oxford University Press, 2002), esp. ch. 4.

19. *The Division of Labour in Society* (1893); English translation (Glencoe, Illinois, The Free Press, 1947).

20. Stanford M. Lyman, 'The Gothic Foundation of Robert E. Park's conception of race and culture' in Luigi Tomasi (ed.), *The Tradition of the Chicago School of Sociology* (Aldershot, Ashgate, 1998), p. 20.

21. *The Elementary Forms of the Religious Life* (1912); English translation (London, George Allen and Unwin, 1915), p. 475.

22. See, for instance, Frank Prochaska, *Christianity and Social Service in Modern Britain: The Disinherited Spirit* (Oxford, Oxford University Press, 2006).

23. See Christopher Parker, *The English Historical Tradition since 1850* (Edinburgh, John Donald, 1990), pp. 44–8; and Peter Hinchliff, *God and History* (Oxford, Clarendon, 1992), ch. 1.

24. Speech given on 27 November 2006 at: http://comunities. gov.uk/index.asp?id=1504751

25. See the bids for the European Capital of Culture 2008, Locum Consulting, at: http://www.locumconsulting.com/pdf/LDR9 CapitalOfCulture.pdf, p. 58.

26. On New Labour's love-affair with Tuscany see, for instance, Rachel Sylvester, 'New Labour heads for Tuscany while old guard stays at home', in *The Daily Telegraph* , 17 July 1997; and Julian Glover, 'Let Tuscan Tony do it in style' in *The Guardian*, 8 August 2000, at: http://www.guardian.co.uk/politics/2000/aug/08/ tonyblair.uk1

27. Cited on 'Alcohol Alert' website, entry on The Licensing Act at: http://www.ias.org.uk/resources/publications/alcoholalert/alert 200501/al200501_p2.html

28. This was outlined in the policy document by Lord Filkin *et al.* on behalf of the New Local Government Network, *Towards a New Localism* (London, NLGN, 2000).

29. On this see, Tony Travers, 'Local Government' in Anthony Seldon, *Blair's Britain* (Cambridge, Cambridge University Press, 2007), pp. 54–78, esp. pp. 64–7; and Lawrence Pratchett, 'Local Autonomy, Local Democracy and the "New Localism"', in *Political Studies* 52 (2004), pp. 358–75.

30. Ruth Kelly, July 2006 from Departmental website at http://www.communities.gov.uk/index.asp?id=1501559

31. Hazel Blears from the Departmental website at: http://www. communities.gov.uk/statements/corporate/statement-blears

32. Mission Statement on Departmental website at: http://www. communities.gov.uk/index.asp?id=1500185

33. At: http://www.communities.gov.uk/pub/98/StrongandProsper ousCommunitiestheLocalGovernmentWhitePaperVol1_id15040 98.pdf; Summary at: http://www.communities.gov.uk/pub/100/ StrongandProsperousCommunitiestheLocalGovernmentWhite PaperSummary_id1504100.pdf

34. See Simon Lee, *Best for Britain: The Politics and Legacy of Gordon Brown* (Oxford, Oneworld, 2007), ch. 4.

35. See Tony Travers, 'Local Government', op. cit., pp. 54–78.

36. Anthony King, *The British Constitution* (Oxford, Oxford University Press, 2007), p. 151.

37. Ibid., p. 177.

38. See Mark D. Chapman, *Bishops, Saints and Politics* (London, T. & T. Clark, 2007), ch. 1.

Chapter 3: Brown, Britishness and Community

1. On Gordon Brown, see esp. Simon Lee, *Best for Britain? The Politics and Legacy of Gordon Brown* (Oxford, Oneworld, 2007); and Robert Peston, *Brown's Britain* (London, Short Books, 2006).

2. See Tom Bentley, 'Learning to let go: The potential of a self-creating society' in Gerry Hassan (ed.), *After Blair: Politics after the New Labour Decade* (London, Lawrence and Wishart, 2007), pp. 94–106, here p. 101.

3. Gordon Brown, speech to the 2006 Labour Party Conference at Manchester, at: http://www.guardian.co.uk/politics/2006/sep/ 25/labourconference.labour2

4. Simon Lee, *Best for Britain?*, op. cit., p. 4.

5. Hazel Blears, 5 July 2007 at: http://www.communities.gov. uk/speeches/corporate/conference2007

6. Pratchett, 'Local Autonomy, Local Democracy and the "New Localism"', pp. 372–3.

7. *Making Assets Work* (London, DCLG, 2007) at: http://www. communities.gov.uk/documents/communities/pdf/321083

8. Ibid., p. 7.

9. See also Emily Thornberry, Rick Muir and Ian Kearns, 'Power Politics: Who runs Britain?', in Nick Pearce and Julia Margo (eds.), *Politics for a New Generation* (London, Palgrave Macmillan, 2007), pp. 279–302, esp. p. 295.

10. Hazel Blears, 'Bringing Devolution to Life', 18 September 2007 at: http://www.communities.gov.uk/speeches/corporate/bring-ingdevolution

11. Hazel Blears, 'Confident Communities', 17 September 2007 at: http://www.communities.gov.uk/speeches/corporate/ confidentcommunities

12. Community anchors are defined as community-led organisations,

which are 'multi-purpose and provide holistic solutions to local problems and challenges, bringing out the best in people and agencies. They are there for the long term, not just the quick fix. Community anchors are often the driving force in community renewal'. See: http://www.communitymatters.org.uk/docs/ Community_anchors_leaflet.pdf

13. *The Governance of Britain* (London, HMSO, 2007) at: http://www.officialdocuments.gov.uk/document/cm71/7170/7 170.pdf

14. G. D. H. Cole, *Socialism and Fascism, 1931–1939* (A History of Socialist Thought, Vol. V) (New York, St Martin's Press, 1960), p. 337.

15. On Cole, see Marc Stears, *Progressives, Pluralists, and the Problems of the State: Ideologies of Reform in the United States and Britain, 1909–1926* (Oxford, Oxford University Press, 2002), ch. 5.

16. *An Action Plan for Community Empowerment: Building on Success* (London, DCLG, 2007) at: http://www.communities.gov.uk/ documents/communities/pdf/actionplan

17. http://www.communities.gov.uk/speeches/corporate/community empowerment

18. *An Action Plan for Community Empowerment*, op. cit., p. 3.

19. Ibid., p. 8.

20. Ibid., pp. 44–5.

21. Ibid., pp. 13, 20, 30.

22. Ibid., p. 20.

23. 12 December 2007 at: http://www.communities.gov.uk/speeches/ corporate/lgaassembly

24. See http://www.communityplanning.net/methods/method 100.htm

25. Concordat between Central Government and the LGA, 12 December 2007 at: http://www.communities.gov.uk/documents/ localgovernment/pdf/601000

26. 22 January 2008, 'A New Deal for Local Devolution?' at: http://www.communities.gov.uk/speeches/corporate/local devolution

27. *Unlocking the Talent of our Communities* (London, DCLG, 2008) at: http://www.communities.gov.uk/documents/communities/ pdf/712089

28. Ibid., p. 8.

29. 19 March 2008, at: http://www.communities.gov.uk/speeches/ corporate/communityengagement

30. Simon Lee, *Best for Britain?*, op. cit., p. 38.

31. On this, see D. Osborne and T. Gabeler, *Re-inventing Government: How the Entrepreneurial Spirit is Transforming the Public Sector*

(Reading, Mass., Addison-Wesley, 1992).

32. Ibid., p. 35.
33. Simon Lee, *Best for Britain?*, op. cit., p. 111.
34. Gordon Brown, 'State and Market: Towards a Public Interest Test' in *Political Quarterly* 74 (2003), pp. 266–84, here p. 282.
35. Ibid., p. 283.
36. Ibid., p. 284.
37. On this, see, for instance, A. Pollock, *NHS plc: The Privatisation of our Health Care* (London, Verso, 2005).
38. Gordon Brown, 'Remarks at 21st Century Public Services: Putting People First', 6 June 2006 at: http://www.hm-treasury.gov.uk/newsroom_and_speeches/press/2006/press_39_06.cfm
39. Gordon Brown, Presentation at the Public Service Reform Conference, 'Learning from front line', 27 March 2007 at: http://www.hm-treasury.gov.uk/newsroom_and_speeches/speeches/chancellorexchequer/speech_chx_290307.cfm>
40. See Anthony King, *The British Constitution* (Oxford, Oxford University Press, 2007), p. 179.
41. Simon Lee, *Best for Britain?*, op. cit., ch. 2.
42. On this, see the impressive and entertaining account by Christopher G. A. Bryant, *The Nations of Britain* (Oxford, Oxford University Press, 2006).
43. Tony Blair, 'The Duty to Integrate: Shared British Values' (speech given at Downing Street to an event hosted by the Runnymede Trust) at: http://www.number10.gov.uk/output/Page10563.asp
44. Gordon Brown has continued in similar vein and has spoken of 'mandatory English training' ('Who do we want to be? The future of Britishness', 14 January 2006 at: http://fabians.org.uk/events/new-year-conference-06/brown-britishness/speech).
45. 'Blunkett Calls for Honest and Open Debate on Citizenship and Community' (17 December 2001), 10 Downing Street Newsroom at: http://www.number-10.gov.uk/news. xasp?news ID=3255
46. Gordon Brown, *Spectator*/Allied Dunbar Lecture, 4 November 1997 at: http://www3.clearlight.com/~acsa/journal/speclect.htm
47. This theme was repeated in the lecture given at the Smith Institute on 15 April 1999 at: http://www.hmtreasury.gov.uk/newsroom_and_speeches/speeches/chancellorexchequer/speech_chex_19990415.cfm
48. Gordon Brown, 'Britishness' (7 July 2004) in *Moving Britain Forward: Selected Speeches 1997–2006* (London, Bloomsbury, 2006), pp. 1–26; also at: http://www.guardian.co.uk/politics/2004/jul/08/ uk.labour

49. Gordon Brown, *Spectator*/Allied Dunbar Lecture, op. cit.
50. This theme was repeated in the lecture to the British Council in 2004.
51. Gordon Brown, 'Who do we want to be? The future of Britishness', op. cit.
52. See, for instance, his contribution to a seminar on Britishness: Gordon Brown, Remarks at a seminar on Britishness, 27 February 2007 at: http://www.hmtreasury.gov.uk/newsroom_and_speeches/speeches/ chancellorexchequer/speech_chx_270207.cfm
53. Ibid.
54. Gordon Brown, 'Who do we want to be? The future of Britishness', op. cit.
55. Linda Colley, *Britons: Forging the Nation, 1707–1837* (New Haven, Yale University Press, 1992).
56. He cites a number of authors by name: Norman Davies, *The Isles: A History* (London, Macmillan, 1999); Tom Nairn, *The Break-up of Britain* (London, NLB, 1977) and *After Britain* (London, Granta, 2000); Simon Heffer, *Nor Shall my Sword: the Reinvention of England* (London, Weidenfeld and Nicolson, 1999); Roger Scruton, *England: An Elegy* (London, Chatto and Windus, 2000).
57. See Jonathan Sacks, *The Dignity of Difference: How to Avoid the Clash of Civilisations* (London, Continuum, revised edn, 2003).
58. Remarks at a Seminar on Britishness, 27 February 2007, op. cit.
59. Gordon Brown, 'Britishness', 7 July 2004, op. cit.
60. Gordon Brown, 'Who do we want to be? The future of Britishness', op. cit.
61. Simon Lee, *Best for Britain?*, op. cit., pp. 145–9.
62. On this see Arthur Aughey, *The Politics of Englishness* (Manchester, Manchester University Press, 2007), ch. 1; and Christopher G. A. Bryant, *The Nations of Britain*, op. cit., ch. 1.

Chapter 4: Religion and Community Cohesion

1. This was the focus of the 1968 Race Relations Act which did not recognise religion as a separate form of identity.
2. See below, ch. 5.
3. Tariq Modood, *Multiculturalism* (Cambridge, Polity, 2007), p. 70. See also p. 30.
4. Amartya Sen, *Identity and Violence* (London, Allen Lane, 2006), p. 165.
5. Grace Davie, *Religion in Britain since 1945: Believing without Belonging* (Oxford, Blackwell, 1994), p. 26.
6. Bhikhu Parekh, *Rethinking Multiculturalism: Cultural Diversity and Political Thinking* (Basingstoke, Palgrave Macmillan, 2nd edn, 2006), p. 198.

7. See Grace Davie, *Sociology of Religion* (London, Sage, 2007), pp. 175–7.

8. See Welmoet Boender and Meryem Kanmaz, 'Imams in the Netherlands and Islam Teachers in Flanders' in Wasf Shadid and Sjoerd van Koningsveld (eds.), *Intercultural Relations and Religious Authorities: Muslims in the European Union* (Leuven, Peeters, 2002), pp. 169–80, esp. p. 171.

9. Trevor Phillips, 'After 7/7: Sleepwalking to Segregation' (speech given at Manchester Town Hall, 22 September 2005) at: http://83.137.212.42/sitearchive/cre/Default.aspx.LocIDohgnew 07s.RefLocID-ohg00900c002.Lang-EN.htm

10. Commission for Racial Equality Corporate Plan, 2006–7, p. 13 at: http://www.equalityhumanrights.com/Documents/CRE/PDF/cre-corporate-plan-2006-2009.pdf

11. John Rex, 'Urban Segregation in Great Britain', in Ceri Peach, Vaughan Robinson and Susan Smith (eds.), *Ethnic Segregation in Cities* (London, Croom Helm, 1981), pp. 25–42, here p. 31.

12. The work of the ICTF has been analysed by Jenny Taylor in 'British Government and the Inner Cities' in Grace Davie, Paul Heelas and Linda Woodhead (eds.), *Predicting Religion* (Aldershot, Ashgate, 2003), pp. 120–32.

13. Jenny Taylor, 'British Government', op. cit., p. 129. See José Casanova, *Public Religions in the Modern World* (Chicago, Chicago University Press, 1994).

14. For a brief overview, see Grace Davie, *Religion in Modern Europe* (Oxford, Oxford University Press, 2000), pp. 126–30.

15. Tariq Modood, 'Reflections on the Rushdie Affair: Muslims, Race and Equality in Britain' in *Multicultural Politics* (Edinburgh, Edinburgh University Press, 2007), pp. 103–112.

16. See Tariq Modood, 'Multiculturalism, Secularism, and the State', in *Multicultural Politics*, op. cit., pp. 131–50, esp. p. 131.

17. Charles Taylor, 'Multiculturalism and "the politics of recognition"' in A. Gutman (ed.), *Multiculturalism and "the politics of recognition"* (Princeton, Princeton University Press, 1994), p. 62.

18. On the history of this term in relation to the 'riots' of 2001, see Paul Bagguley and Yasmin Hussain, 'Conflict and Cohesion: constructions of "community" around the 2001 "riots"' (lecture to 2003 Communities Conference) at: http://www.leeds.ac.uk/sociology/people/pbdocs/Conflict%20and%20Cohesion%204%20conference.doc

19. On Bradford, see Herman Ouseley, *Community Pride, Not Prejudice: Making Diversity Work in Practice* (Bradford, Bradford Vision, 2001); on Burnley, see Anthony Clarke, *Burnley Task Force Report* (Burnley, Burnley Task Force, 2001); on Oldham, see David

Ritchie, *Oldham Independent Review Panel Report* (Manchester, Government Office for the North-west, 2001); John Denham, *Building Cohesive Communities: A Report of the Ministerial Group on Public Order and Community Cohesion* (London, Home Office, 2001); and Ted Cantle, *Community Cohesion: A Report of the Independent Review Team Chaired by Ted Cantle* (London, Home Office, 2001) at: http://image.guardian.co.uk/sys-files/Guardian/documents/2001/12/11/communitycohesionreport.pdf

20. See Ted Cantle, *Community Cohesion: A New Framework for Race and Diversity* (Basingstoke, Palgrave, 2005), p. 52.

21. Ted Cantle, *Community Cohesion: A Report of the Independent Review Team*, op. cit., p. 72.

22. For an insightful critique of the construction of identity in the Cantle report, see Paul Bagguley and Yasmin Hussain, 'Flying the Flag for England? Citizenship, Religion and Cultural Identity among British Pakistani Muslims' in Tahir Abbas (ed.), *Muslim Britain: Communities under Pressure* (London, Zed Books, 2005), pp. 222–33.

23. Speech given on 27 November 2006 at: http://communities.gov.uk/index.asp?id=1504751

24. At: http://www.communities.gov.uk/communities/racecohesion faith/communitycohesion/

25. See, for instance, *Community Cohesion Standards for Schools* at: http://www.standards.dfes.gov.uk/pdf/commcohesion.pdf

26. *'What works' in Community Cohesion* (London, DCLG, 2007) at: http://www.communities.gov.uk/documents/communities/pdf/whatworks

27. *Our Shared Future* at: http://www.integrationandcohesion.org.uk/Our_final_report.aspx

28. Ibid., p. 10.

29. See Hannah Jones, 'Faith in Community', *eSharp* Issue 7, pp. 11–13 at: http://www.sharp.arts.gla.ac.uk/issue7/Jones.pdf

30. See Michael Keith, *Riots, Race and Policing: Lore and Disorder in a Multi-Racial Society* (London, UCL Press, 1993).

31. Amartya Sen, *Identity and Violence*, op. cit., p. 14.

32. Report chaired by Bhikhu Parekh for the Commission for Multi-Ethnic Britain, *The Future of Multi-Ethnic Britain* (London, Profile Books, 2000), §4.19.

33. Sen, *Identity and Violence*, op. cit., p. 4.

34. See Frederick Medis (ed.), *The Church of Ceylon: A History 1945–1995* (Colombo, Diocese of Ceylon, 1995).

35. On this, see Nira Wickramasinghe, *Sri Lanka in the Modern Age: A History of Contested Identities* (Colombo, Vijitha Yapa Publications, 2006), esp. Part 1.

36. *Our Shared Future*, op. cit., §2.50.

37. Ibid., e.g. §§ 4.11, 4.41, 8.3.

38. Ibid., §8.4.

39. For a detailed critique of social capital in relation to community cohesion, see Derek McGhee, 'Moving to "our" common ground – a critical examination of community cohesion discourse in twenty-first century Britain' in *The Sociological Review* 51 (2003), pp. 376–404.

40. *Our Shared Future*, op. cit., §11.

41. Office of the Deputy Prime Minister, *Sustainable Communities: People, Places and Prosperity. A Five Year Plan from the office of the Deputy Prime Minister* (London, HMSO, 2005), p. 18 at: http://www.communities.gov.uk/pub/490/SustainableCommun itiesPeoplePlacesandProsperity_id1500490.pdf; see also Tony Travers, 'Local Government' in Anthony Seldon, *Blair's Britain* (Cambridge, Cambridge University Press, 2007), pp. 67–8.

42. At: http://www.communities.gov.uk/pub/98/Strongand ProsperousCommunitiestheLocalGovernmentWhitePaperVol1_i d1504098.pdf; Summary at: http://www.communities.gov.uk/ pub/100/ StrongandProsperousCommunitiestheLocalGovern mentWhitePaperSummary_id1504100.pdf

43. 'Local Strategic Partnerships are statutory, multi-agency partner-ships, which matches [*sic*] local authority boundaries. LSPs bring together at a local level the different parts of the public, private, community and voluntary sectors; allowing different initiatives and services to support one another so that they can work togeth-er more effectively', at: http://www.neighbourhood.gov.uk/ page.asp?id=531

44. *Community Cohesion: An Action Guide* (London, Local Government Association, 2004).

45. Ibid., p. 10.

46. Office of the Deputy Prime Minister, *Sustainable Communities*, op. cit., p. 24.

47. Ian Bradley has even given this idea a rather dubious Trinitarian interpretation: see *Believing in Britain* (London, I. B. Tauris, 2007), p. 27.

48. Derek McGhee, 'Moving to "our" common ground', op. cit., p. 400.

49. §§4.27, 4.28.

50. Tony Blair, 'The Duty to Integrate: Shared British Values' (speech given at Downing Street to an event hosted by the Runnymede Trust) at: http://www.number10.gov.uk/output/ Page10563.asp

Chapter 5: Rowan Williams and the Politics
of Interactive Pluralism

1. 'Civil and Religious Law in England: a Religious Perspective', Royal Courts of Justice, 7 February 2008. Text at: http://www.archbishopofcanterbury.org/1575

2. For various criticisms see: http://www.telegraph.co.uk/news/main.jhtml?xml=/news/2008/02/07/nwilliams407.xml

3. At: http://www.ramadhanfoundation.com/williamssharia.htm

4. George Carey, 'Are we promoting harmony or Muslim ghettoes?' in *The Sunday Telegraph*; the *News of the World* article had no title. Both appeared on 10 February 2008.

5. *The Guardian*, 9 February 2008.

6. See his speech on Christianophobia at: http://www.markpritchard.com/search/article.php?id=927

7. Rowan Williams, 'Liberation Theology and the Anglican Tradition' in Rowan Williams and David Nicholls (eds.), *Politics and Theological Identity: Two Anglican Essays* (London, The Jubilee Group, 1984), pp. 7–26, here p. 17.

8. Williams, 'Liberation Theology and the Anglican Tradition', op. cit., p. 18.

9. Paul Avis, *Anglicanism and the Christian Church* (London, T. & T. Clark, 2002).

10. On this, see Harold Laski's fascinating remarks about establishment in *Political Thought in England from Locke to Bentham* (London, Williams and Norgate, 1920): '"Thoughtful men," the Archbishop of Canterbury has told the House of Lords, "… see the absolute need, if a Church is to be strong and vigorous, for the Church, *qua* church, to be able to say what it can do as a church." "The rule of the sovereign, the rule of Parliament," replied Lord Haldane, "extend as far as the rule of the Church. They are not to be distinguished or differentiated, and that was the condition under which ecclesiastical power was transmitted to the Church of England." To-day, that is to say, as in the past, antithetic theories of the nature of the State hinge, in essence, upon the problem of its sovereignty. "A free church in a free state," now, as then, may be our ideal; but we still seek the means wherewith to build it' (p. 85).

11. Figgis was the one person mentioned as an influence by Williams in a lengthy interview with the *Church Times* (29 November 2002).

12. On Figgis, see my *Bishops, Saints and Politics: Anglican Studies* (London, T. & T. Clark, 2007), ch. 4; and *Blair's Britain* (London, DLT, 2005), pp. 84–92.

13. Williams, 'Liberation Theology and the Anglican Tradition', op. cit., p. 21.

14. On Figgis and conciliarism, see my essay, 'The Dull Bits of History: Cautionary Tales for Anglicanism' in Mark D. Chapman (ed.), *The Anglican Covenant: Unity and Diversity in the Anglican Communion* (London, Mowbray, 2008), pp. 81–99.

15. Williams, 'Liberation Theology and the Anglican Tradition', op. cit., p. 22.

16. See also 'The Trinity and Pluralism' in *On Christian Theology* (Oxford, Blackwell, 2000), pp. 167–80.

17. The rising influence of other religions was scarcely noted in the influential report of the Archbishop of Canterbury's Commission on Urban Priority Areas, *Faith in the City: a Call for Action by Church and Nation* (London, Church House Publishing, 1985).

18. 'Religion, Culture, Diversity and Tolerance: Shaping the New Europe', 8 November 2005. Posted at: http://www.anglican communion.org/acns/news.cfm/2005/11/8/ACNS4068

19. 'Law, Power and Peace: Christian Perspectives on Sovereignty', 25 September 2005, at: http://www.dnmt.org.uk/dnmt/images/docs/dnmlecture_2005.pdf

20. Nicholls wrote widely on pluralism. See David Nicholls, *The Pluralist State* (London, Macmillan, 2nd edn, 1994) and 'Authority in Church and State aspects of the thought of J. N. Figgis and his contemporaries' (unpublished Cambridge PhD diss., 1962). See more recently the excellent book by Marc Stears, *Progressives, Pluralists, and the Problems of the State: Ideologies of Reform in the United States and Britain, 1909–1926* (Oxford, Oxford University Press, 2002).

21. 'Law, Power and Peace', op. cit., p. 1.

22. Ibid., p. 3.

23. Ibid., p. 2.

24. Ibid., p. 4.

25. Ibid., p. 9.

26. Ibid., pp. 7–8.

27. Ibid., p. 5.

28. Ibid., pp. 7–8.

29. Ibid., pp. 8–9.

30. 'The Unity of Christian Truth' in *On Christian Theology*, op. cit., pp. 16–28, 17.

31. 'Law, Power and Peace', op. cit., p. 9.

32. 'Europe, Faith and Culture', speech given at Liverpool, 26 January 2008. Posted at: http://www.archbishopofcanterbury.org/1547

33. 'Law, Power and Peace', op. cit., p. 7.

34. Lecture given on 12 May 2007 at St Andrew's Cathedral,

Singapore: 'Christianity: Public Religion and the Common Good'. Posted at: http://www.archbishopofcanterbury.org/495

35. 'The Incarnation as the Basis for Dogma' in Robert Morgan (ed.), *The Religion of the Incarnation* (Bristol, Bristol Classical Press, 1989), pp. 85–98, 89.

36. 'What is Catholic Orthodoxy?' in Kenneth Leech and Rowan Williams (eds.), *Essays Catholic and Radical* (London, Bowardean, 1983), pp. 11–25, here p. 25. The criticism of political power is a major theme of this essay.

37. 'Convictions, Loyalties and the Secular State', Chatham Lecture, 29 October 2004. At: http://www.archbishopofcanterbury.org/1478. See also 'The Judgement of the World' in *On Christian Theology*, op. cit., p. 35.

38. 'Religion, Culture, Diversity and Tolerance', op. cit.

39. 'Europe, Faith and Culture', op. cit.

40. 'The Unity of Christian Truth', op. cit., p. 17.

41. 'Europe, Faith and Culture', op. cit.

42. 'Religion, Culture, Diversity and Tolerance', op. cit.

43. Michael Nazir-Ali, 'Extremism flourished as UK lost Christianity', *Sunday Telegraph*, 11 January 2008.

44. 'The Unity of Christian Truth', op. cit., p. 17.

45. 'Law, Power and Peace', op. cit., p. 4.

46. 'Convictions, Loyalties and the Secular State', op. cit.

47. 'Religion, Culture, Diversity and Tolerance', op. cit.

48. Presidential address to November 2005 synod.

Chapter 6: Islam, the Archbishop and the Future

1. 'Civil and Religious Law in England: a Religious Perspective', Royal Courts of Justice, 7 February 2008. Text at: http://www.archbishopofcanterbury.org/1575

2. Donald MacKinnon, 'Kenosis and Establishment' in *The Stripping of the Altars* (London, Fontana, 1969), pp. 13–40, here p. 34.

3. In his first press conference in April 2005 following his election, Pope Benedict XV spoke of the 'inalienable Christian roots of [European] culture and civilization'.

4. See 'The Judgement of the World' in *On Christian Theology* (Oxford, Blackwell, 2000), p. 35.

5. George Carey, 'Are we promoting harmony or Muslim ghettoes?' in *The Sunday Telegraph*, 10 February 2008.

6. 'Civil and Religious Law in England', op. cit.

7. 'Convictions, Loyalties and the Secular State', Chatham Lecture, 29 October 2004. At: http://www.archbishopofcanterbury.org/1478

8. Citing Tariq Ramadan, *Western Muslims and the Future of Islam* (Oxford, Oxford University Press, 2004), pp. 53, 55.

9. 'Religion, Culture, Diversity and Tolerance: Shaping the New Europe', 8 November 2005. Posted at: http://www.anglican communion.org/acns/news.cfm/2005/11/8/ACNS4068

10. See also Ron Greaves, 'Negotiating British Citizenship and Muslim Identity' in Tahir Abbas (ed.), *Muslim Britain: Communities under Pressure* (London, Zed Books, 2005), pp. 66–77.

11. 10 February 2008.

12. Amartya Sen offers a vigorous critique of faith-based education: 'In Britain a confounded view of what a multiethnic society must do has led to encouraging the development of state-financed Muslim schools, Hindu schools, Sikh schools, etc., to supplement preexisting state-supported Christian schools, and young children are powerfully placed in the domain of singular affiliations well before they have the ability to reason about different systems of identification that may compete for their attention' (*Identity and Violence*, [London, Allen Lane, 2006], p. 13). But see also Anthony Giddens, *Over to You, Mr Brown* (Cambridge, Polity, 2007), p. 160.

13. 'Civil and Religious Law in England', op. cit.

14. 'Law, Power and Peace: Christian Perspectives on Sovereignty', 25 September 2005, at: http://www.dnmt.org.uk/dnmt/images/ docs/dnmlecture_2005.pdf, p. 8.

15. Tony Blair, 'The Duty to Integrate: Shared British Values' (speech given at Downing Street to an event hosted by the Runnymede Trust) at: http://www.number10.gov.uk/output/Page10563.asp

16. On this, see Matthew Grimley, *Citizenship, Community, and the Church of England: Liberal Anglican Theories of the State Between the Wars* (Oxford, Clarendon Press, 2004), ch. 2.

17. I attempted something similar in my *Blair's Britain: A Christian Critique* (London, DLT, 2005), esp. ch. 7.

18. For a critique of multicultural theories which downplay the importance of religion, see Tariq Modood, *Multiculturalism: A Civic Idea* (Cambridge, Polity, 2007), esp. p. 30.

19. Trevor Phillips, 'After 7/7: Sleepwalking to Segregation' (speech given at Manchester Town Hall, 22 September 2005) at: http:// www.cre.gov.uk/Default.aspx.LocID-0hgnew07r.RefLocID-0h g00900c001001.Lang-EN.htm

20. Ian Bradley, *Believing in Britain* (London, I. B. Tauris, 2007), esp. ch. 6.

21. Chandran Kukathas, *The Liberal Archipelago: A Theory of Diversity and Freedom* (Oxford, Oxford University Press, 2003), pp. 8–9.

22. Ibid., p. 15. Cf. p. 19.

23. Ibid., p. 19.

24. Ibid., p. 31.

25. Tariq Modood, *Multiculturalism: A Civic Idea*, op. cit., p. 37.

26. Ibid., p. 43.
27. Anthony Giddens, *Over to You, Mr Brown*, op. cit., p. 155.
28. See Charles Taylor, *Multiculturalism: Examining the Politics of Recognition* (Princeton, Princeton University Press, 1994).
29. 'Convictions, Loyalties and the Secular State', op. cit. Citing Maleiha Malik, 'Muslims and Participatory Democracy', in Mohammad Siddique Seddon, Dilwar Hussain and Nadeem Malik (eds.), *British Muslims: Loyalty and Belonging* (Islamic Foundation, London, Citizen Organising Foundation, 2003), pp. 69–85:'Institutional identification is more likely where substantive issues concerning the common good are discussed' (p. 80).
30. 'Convictions, Loyalties and the Secular State', op. cit. See also 'The Judgement of the World', op. cit., p. 37.

Chapter 7: Conclusion

1. Matthew Grimley, *Citizenship, Community, and the Church of England: Liberal Anglican Theories of the State Between the Wars* (Oxford, Clarendon Press, 2004), p. 225.
2. 'Theology in the Public Arena:The Case of English Bonhoefferism' in Jane Garnett, Matthew Grimley, Alana Harris, William Whyte and Sarah Williams (eds.), *Redefining Christian Britain: Post 1945 Perspectives* (London, SCM Press, 2007), pp. 92–105.
3. *The God Delusion* (London, Black Swan, 2007).
4. *God is not Great: How Religion Poisons Everything* (New York, Atlantic, 2008).
5. Colin Crouch, *Post-Democracy* (Cambridge, Polity, 2004).
6. See Tom Bentley, 'Learning to let go: The potential of a self-creating society' in Gerry Hassan (ed.), *After Blair: Politics after the New Labour Decade* (London, Lawrence and Wishart, 2007), pp. 94–106, here p. 100.
7. The Report from the Commission on Urban Life and Faith, *Faithful Cities: A Call for Celebration, Vision and Justice* (London, Church House Publishing and Peterborough, Methodist Publishing House, 2006), §§1.11–1.16.
8. Ibid., §5.34.
9. Ibid., §5.36.
10. Ibid., §§7.62–7.68.
11. Ibid., §7.47.
12. This seems to me to be a serious problem affecting Andrew Bradstock's otherwise laudable vision for community action through the churches in *Louder than Words: Action for the 21st-century Church* (London, DLT, 2007).
13. See Anthony Giddens, *Over to You, Mr Brown* (Cambridge, Polity, 2007), p. 155.

14. Paul Bagguley and Yasmin Hussain, 'Flying the Flag for England? Citizenship, Religion and Cultural Identity among British Pakistani Muslims' in Tahir Abbas (ed.), *Muslim Britain: Communities under Pressure* (London, Zed Books, 2005), pp. 222–33, here p. 213.
15. Giddens, *Over to You, Mr Brown*, op. cit., ch. 7. See also Amartya Sen, *Identity and Violence* (London, Allen Lane, 2006), pp. 158–65.
16. On this, see Charles Taylor, *Multiculturalism: Examining the Politics of Recognition* (Princeton, Princeton University Press, 1994).
17. Giddens, *Over to You, Mr Brown*, op. cit., p. 156.
18. Sue Goss, 'Re-imagining the public realm' in Hassan (ed.), *After Blair*, op. cit., pp. 107–19, esp. pp. 114–15.
19. *The Acquisitive Society* (London, G. Bell, 1921), p. 8.

Bibliography

1. The many internet references to lectures and Government documents are included in the Notes section of this book.

INDEX